Praise for *More Love, Less Conflict*

"*More Love, Less Conflict* is brimming with wonderful ideas and methods that can help any couple experience a deeper, more profound connection."
    —John Gray, author of *Men Are from Mars, Women Are from Venus*

"*More Love, Less Conflict* will give you just that: more love. It rests on the premise that love is not just something we feel from time to time (if we are lucky) but is also something we can cultivate and get better at through conscious practice. This book is full of practical tools that you can use to generate more love in your life."
    —Arjuna Ardagh, author of *Radical Brilliance* and *The Translucent Revolution*

"Jonathan has created a wonderful resource to help us all improve our communication and understand each other better. If we all applied these ideas in our relationships, the world would be a far more peaceful place!"
    —Lori Deschene, author of *Tiny Buddha's Gratitude Journal* and other books, creator of the website *tinybuddha.com*

"*More Love, Less Conflict* is the book that provides all the real and effective shortcuts to live a life of deep connection with your mate, your family, and even your friends. If you want to get more of what you want in life—more love, more intimacy, and less difficulty—this book can help get you there."

—Peter Sandhill, facilitator, Human Awareness Institute

"Engaging, illuminating, and accessible. *More Love, Less Conflict* is full of practical ideas and powerful exercises for any couple seeking to strengthen their communication and deepen their connection."

—Suzann Pileggi Pawelski, MAPP and James O. Pawelski, PhD, coauthors of *Happy Together: Using the Science of Positive Psychology to Build Love That Lasts*

MORE LOVE
Less
Conflict

—— A ——

Communication Playbook
for Couples

JONATHAN ROBINSON

author of *Communication Miracles for Couples*

Conari Press

This edition first published in 2018 by Conari Press, an imprint of
Red Wheel/Weiser, LLC
With offices at:
65 Parker Street, Suite 7
Newburyport, MA 01950
www.redwheelweiser.com

ISBN: 978-1-57324-727-6

Library of Congress Cataloging-in-Publication Data

Names: Robinson, Jonathan, 1959- author.
Title: More love, less conflict : a communication playbook for couples /
   Jonathan Robinson.
Description: Newburyport, MA : Conari Press, 2018. | Includes bibliograph-
ical references and index.
Identifiers: LCCN 2018000897 | ISBN 9781573247276 (pbk. : alk. paper)
Subjects: LCSH: Couples--Psychology. | Man-woman relationships. |
   Interpersonal communication. | Interpersonal relations.
Classification: LCC HQ801 .R595 2018 | DDC 306.7--dc23
LC record available at https://lccn.loc.gov/2018000897

Cover design by Kathryn Sky-Peck
Cover photograph © Exactostock-1527 / Shutterstock
Interior by Jane Hagaman
Typeset in Sabon and Avenir

Printed in Canada
MAR
10 9 8 7 6 5 4 3 2 1

Contents

Introduction

For over thirty years, I've been a therapist with a focus on providing clients with practical tools they can use immediately at home. Most couples aren't interested in dredging up childhood issues in long months of therapy. Instead, they want effective ways to sidestep arguments, handle ongoing challenges, or once again enjoy the love and connection they knew at the beginning of their relationship.

When we share deeply satisfying and intimate moments with our partners, it gives our lives joy and meaning. The problem is that most couples don't know how to create such moments *consistently*. With the pace and myriad distractions of modern life, many couples find the connection they crave is crowded out by their "to-do" lists. Furthermore, when disagreements erupt, they often get lost in blame and don't know how to climb out of the hole they're in. That's when a good strategy or helpful idea can be a lifesaver. With the right information, you can quickly find your way back to your shared loving heart.

I've seen hundreds of couples go through difficult times. I've seen the new challenges they face in this age of social media, constant change, and harried lives. Fortunately, there's good news. Each year, researchers learn new and better ways to help couples get back to the love they really want. With the methods and ideas in this book, you and your partner can quickly find the path to more love and less conflict.

You may be wondering: What's a "communication *playbook*"? A playbook is a book of strategies to help you achieve a certain goal. In terms of relationships, the goal is simple: to experience more love and less conflict. With effective strategies, you can create moments of intimacy, depth, and connection whenever you desire.

Robert and Claire entered my office looking as if they couldn't stand sitting in the same building together, much less on the same couch. When I asked Claire what had brought them to counseling, she launched into a tirade about how she was married to "a lying, conniving, self-absorbed, good-for-nothing jerk." Robert's assessment of his mate was even *less* kind. Evidently, the animosity between them had been building for years. But by teaching them some of the techniques you'll learn in this book, by the end of the hour, they were lovingly holding hands. They had miraculously dropped their anger and blame and were back in love. That's what can happen when couples learn to communicate effectively.

In part 1, I begin by outlining how to create a strong foundation on which love and connection can be built and flourish. Knowing how to communicate effectively is one of the most important skills you can learn in life. Besides impacting the success of your intimate relationships, this one skill also helps determine how well you relate to your kids, your friends, your family, and even how much money you make in your career. According to a famous Harvard study, the best predictor of the quality of people's health and the level of their happiness is the quality of their relationships. So, congratulations for picking up this book!

In part 2, I introduce techniques that will help you to understand your partner better. Understanding is the key to relationship harmony. I have never had a couple enter my office and state: "We understand each other really well; that's why we want a divorce." When couples truly understand each other, the likelihood of conflict is dramatically reduced. The exercises given in part 2 can help you discover many new, helpful, and valuable things about your partner.

In part 3, you'll read about various methods and ideas for increasing love in your relationship. In these chapters, you'll find structured exercises for dramatically increasing the positive connection and intimacy you have with your partner. Even if you choose not to do the structured techniques outlined here, just reading about them will help you feel more intimate with your mate. At the end of each of these chapters, I offer simple and easy practices for creating more fun and affection in your relationship. In fact, these simple practices can be done with anyone at any time, and they can help you create heartfelt moments of connection throughout your daily life.

In part 4, we'll examine communication methods specifically geared toward reducing conflict and helping couples get through rough times. These can save you a lot of money by helping you avoid divorce court or a year in a therapist's office! More important, they can help you quickly resolve conflicts so that you can actually get back to the love and fun you really want in your relationship.

In the Conclusion, I offer some final words of advice. At the back of the book, you'll find appendices that can help you locate and review all the exercises presented. My hope is that you will use these as a quick reference guide when you face a conflict or need to build intimacy with your partner.

For those readers who don't currently have a partner, or have a partner who is unwilling to join them in these practices, I have good news. Unlike dancing, where it takes two skilled people to tango, it does *not* take two skilled people to communicate well. A single skilled partner can often create more love and less conflict by using the practices and principles given in this book. I give specific tips on "flying solo" in chapter 5.

I think you'll find that most of what I have to say here makes intuitive sense to you. However, you may find that the first time you use a method from this book it feels a bit awkward. Whenever we try something new, it can feel like that. Yet, once you see how quickly these methods work, I think you'll be convinced. All I ask is that you try them out—like a new coat—and see if they fit. Use what works for you and discard what feels like an awkward fit or not applicable to your situation. If you do that, I know you'll be pleased with the results you get.

Getting the Most Out of This Book

To get the most out of this book, you should first read completely through part 1. Then feel free to skip to whatever chapters catch your fancy. In each chapter, you'll find practical ideas and easy methods that will improve the quality of your communication forever. And these ideas and methods won't just affect your intimate relationships. The same skills that work with your partner will also work in virtually all your relationships.

In parts 2, 3, and 4, I present distinct communication exercises that provide highly structured ways to communicate with your partner with a desired goal in mind. In addition, at the end of each chapter, I include very simple techniques that you can use in a less formal way. In a way, all of these methods are like the apps you get on your smartphone—specific tools for accomplishing very precise tasks. When you need directions to a friend's house, you load up a mapping application that may offer you a couple of ways to get there. Once you arrive, however, you don't need the app anymore. In a similar way, when you need a specific type of communication with your partner, the practices in this book will be there to guide you to your desired destination. Use the appendices to help you find what you need. As with smartphone apps, these methods will save you time and energy and be available any time you need them.

All the exercises offered in this book have two common elements: they are deliberate and they are finite. Each one provides a deliberate way to communicate with a positive goal in mind and a clear end in sight. Normally, when we communicate, we're not consciously aware of our goals. So our haphazard words, often motivated by hurt and irritation, rarely lead to the love and understanding we really want. The methods offered here can gently guide you toward a specific beneficial outcome. In addition, they all have a clear beginning and a clear end. Some partners especially appreciate this, because they tend to avoid difficult communications. Knowing there is a clear endpoint helps them enter into conversations about difficult issues. The deliberate and finite structure of these exercises helps partners avoid lecturing each other or dredging up the past.

Throughout the book, I also offer what I call Simple and Easy Practices that can help you turn the more structured exercises described in the chapters into methods you can use easily in your daily life. Although it's best to use the many techniques offered here under ideal circumstances—with a willing partner, with no distractions, and with plenty of time to follow precise guidelines—life can be messy, and partners can feel resistant to too many rules. Moreover, once you understand a method, you may not *need* to use it under ideal circumstances. These simplified practices are intended to encourage you and your partner to use the methods in this book much more frequently.

The structured exercises I offer differ in one important way from the simplified practices given at the end of chapters. The exercises require a bit of setup; the simplified practices do not. By "setup," I mean that the structured exercises require that you describe to your partner what a communication exercise is, why you want to use it, and what the benefit will be for both of you for having done so. The advantage of the more structured exercises is that they can generally go deeper. And, when tension is high, they are better at helping couples to get back to a place of love and harmony. Relationships sometimes take work to get back to a place of love. When you use the structured exercises, you give caring communication your highest priority.

I understand that most couples will gravitate toward the simplified pactices, perhaps skimming over the more structured exercises. Even if you don't choose to follow all the structured exercises, however, it can be helpful to read the full descriptions of them, as well as the transcripts of the couples who have used them. You may find that the more structured methods are worth the extra effort. However, even if you decide to use only the simple practices, you'll come away with a much better understanding of the ultimate goal of each principle described.

Three Levels of Communication

According to the Authentic Relating Community (*authenticworld .integralcenter.org*), all communication can be categorized into three levels: informational, emotional/personal, and relational. The first, or informational, level is what we use most of the time in our daily lives. It includes talk about the weather, our jobs, and what we're doing. This is a necessary mode of communication for getting things done, but it lacks depth and true intimacy.

The next level, emotional/personal communication, involves the sharing of our thoughts, feelings, and desires. Many of the techniques in this book relate to this second level. We tend to avoid this depth of intimacy unless we have ways to make this level of contact easy and safe. Conversations about what we like, hate, want, and feel—as well as vulnerable self-reflection—all fit into this category.

The third level of communication, often referred to as relational, occurs when we talk about what's happening *now*—in the moment—between us and others. This is by far the rarest form of communication. Yet it can be very rewarding, because it immediately creates an atmosphere of depth, presence, and connection that is rarely matched in the other two levels. Studies show that couples who report the highest levels of satisfaction spend much more time in relational communication than other couples.

Here's an example of relational communication: "Listening to you just now, I felt some sadness. I'm imagining it's because I've been wanting more quality time with you. How is that for you to hear?" By revealing in real time what's going on with you and asking for your partner's reaction, you create increased vulnerability, presence, and connection.

By being aware of the three levels of communication, you can master the ability to go quickly from light, superficial conversation to deep, meaningful connection. In part 1, you'll learn the various elements needed to deepen, unlock, and enliven intimate connection with your partner, swiftly and smoothly.

PART I

Building Strong Relationships

If you would be loved, love and be loveable.

BENJAMIN FRANKLIN

You may think you already know what makes for good communication and strong relationships. Most of us tend to think *we* know how to have successful relationships—it's our *partners* that could use some help! Yet skilled communicators can connect with virtually anyone. Because they understand the underlying laws of relationships, they can be flexible in their approach and consistently get the outcomes they desire.

The skills and attitudes that lead to great relationships don't come naturally. You have to really study them and learn them step by step. But if you try some of the approaches and methods presented here, I think you'll find that the results can be truly amazing.

CHAPTER 1

What the World Needs Now

In my many years of experience counseling couples, I've found that what most people want above all else in a relationship are moments of care, understanding, and empathy—I use the acronym CUE. When we feel our partners truly "get us," it feels fantastic. When our partners are upset, we need to take the cue to be on CUE. When our partners feel that we understand their pain or know their joy, they feel loved by us. How sweet that can be. Regrettably, however, such moments are rare in most relationships.

While we all want to feel understood, the way we tend to communicate makes this harder and harder. Even when communicating face to face, people often misunderstand each other. And talking by phone or communicating by text or email makes empathic understanding even more challenging. Yes, emojis can sometimes help, but they certainly don't replace the impact of a lover holding your hand, eyes welling up with tears, as you describe an awful day. We want to know that our partners truly *care*, and we often don't care what they have to say until we feel that they really *do* care.

When people are stressed, they are generally not at their best. After millions of years of evolution, we respond to stress in one of three ways—we fight, we flee, or we freeze. Perhaps you've noticed fighting words coming from your partner when you've given them some simple feedback. Your statement "I don't think that outfit will be appropriate for the party" can be met with vitriol and venom—"Look who's talking. You don't look so great yourself." And the fight is on. Conquer or be conquered. This used to be helpful when faced with a tiger on the plains of Africa 200,000 years ago, but it is not useful when dealing with your mate.

Another way we're conditioned to react to stress is to take flight, or flee. Once again, when facing a tiger, this is an effective strategy. But if you avoid needed conversations in your relationship, those needs don't magically go away. In fact, they can soon pile up into a wall of resentment. The next thing you know, you're paying your hard-earned money to a therapist to avoid an impending divorce. Since the whole point of a partnership is to share love and joy, fleeing is not an effective strategy.

A third survival strategy people fall back on when under stress is simply to freeze. You can see this in other animals as well. When a mouse's life is in danger, it sometimes simply "plays dead," hoping that the cat won't bother it. In my couples counseling practice, I often see partners "numb out," or simply not communicate anything about what they feel or want. Their hope is that, if they appear frozen, their partners won't bother them and will leave them alone. In fact, sometimes this strategy can work. Even when it does "work," however, the results are less than satisfying for both people. Eventually, partners can simply "give up," as all the love that was once in the relationship is replaced by animosity and resentment.

Because people today are dealing with more stress than ever, it's critically important to know how to communicate when under pressure. Unfortunately, our biologically programmed reactions—fight, flee, or freeze—tend to make matters even worse. Just when we need to be at our best, we tend to lose our heads. So what can couples do to avoid these ingrained instinctive reactions? What they need are new communication skills and new mechanisms to make sure they use them.

Even though I teach workshops and write books about communication, when severely stressed, I find that it's easy to forget everything I know. For couples who have much less training than I do, I can imagine it may be nearly impossible to go beyond fight, flight, or freeze responses when faced with a big problem. That's why I've developed tools that can work under even the most stressful conditions. Whether your immediate goal is to connect deeply with your mate or to tackle a thorny issue, you'll find practices in this book that can create miracles.

Currently, about 45 percent of marriages end in divorce—and the failure rate of second and third marriages is even worse. That means people aren't getting better at relationships and communication just through repetition. Most of us have had very little communication training, so our communication skills are weak and ineffective. Learning how to master these skills is a bit like building muscles. The structure of the practices in this book will allow you to build your communication "muscles" in a safe and deliberate manner. Once your communication abilities are well developed, you will no longer need as much structure to get to your desired outcome. You will have the communication strength to handle almost any situation.

Finding the Target

Since care, understanding, and empathy are things that we all want, why are they so hard to get? First, we forget (or don't realize) that empathy and understanding are our true goals. So we often lose track of what the real target is and spend our time, energy, and words in pursuit of other ends. For example, you think that proving your partner wrong will help you to feel good—and indeed, feeling you are right and your partner is wrong can temporarily make you feel very powerful. Yet there's always a price to be paid. It may feel good in the moment to blame our partners and put them down, but the result of such behavior is never more love and less conflict.

Simply having a clearly defined target will get you halfway to your goal of more love. I learned the importance of having a clearly defined target while in college. One day, my roommate challenged me to a game of one-on-one basketball. He was a great basketball player. In fact, he was the only freshman on the varsity team. However, I felt I could use my brain to overcome his talent. I accepted his challenge on one condition—that I be allowed to place a one-ounce object anywhere on the court before the game began. My roommate accepted my terms, and we headed for the court. Once there, I took out my one-ounce object—a blindfold—and placed it in a strategic location—over my roommate's eyes. Then I announced: "Let the games begin!"

Admittedly, it still ended up being a rather close game! But I was able to beat one of the best basketball players around because I knew exactly what the target was—and he did not. Despite my total lack of skill, I found that, if I threw enough balls in the general direction of the basket, sometimes one would go in. In the same way, if you throw enough words in the direction of care, understanding, and empathy, you will occasionally score. You don't need to say the perfect words if you aim for the right target.

The Four Horsemen

Once you know what the right "target" is for good communication, you need to learn what the main obstacles are to hitting that target. There are four distinct culprits that get in the way of expressing care, understanding, and empathy. I refer to them as the Four Horseman of the Relationship Apocalypse: denigration, denial, dismissal, and distraction. When partners engage in any of these behaviors, it foretells that significant problems lie ahead.

Denigration is a way of belittling our partners. The most common way of doing this is through blaming them for all our problems. I see it all the time in my counseling office. Couples blame each other for stupid stuff, like not squeezing the toothpaste from the bottom or shutting the door too loudly. When you denigrate someone, you feel self-righteous or angry, and both of those feelings take you farther away from your goal of emotional connection. In fact, when we use complaint and blame as a strategy to change our partners, it never really works. Instead, it simply keeps us from seeing how *we* may have contributed to the difficulty at hand.

Denial is the second culprit that keeps us from care, understanding, and empathy. When we deny a problem, we don't even recognize that there *is* a problem. Men tend to be better at this than women, but we've all been there. For example, for a long time, I denied that I left dishes in the sink. I eventually learned, however, that denying my role in the conflict did not make the dishes magically disappear. In addition, I learned that denying that I left my dishes in the sink did not do much to appease my wife. In fact, quite the opposite. Denial may seem to work in the short term, but it always comes back to bite you.

The third obstacle to getting what we want in relationships is *dismissal*. When you dismiss or belittle your partner's feelings, you miss an opportunity to show your empathy and care. Even little comments like "You shouldn't feel so upset" or "It's not that big a deal" can make your partner feel misunderstood. The truth is that if our partners feel we don't really understand their feelings, it will be even harder for them to let those feelings go and move on. Frequently, I see men quickly dismiss their partner's feelings and instead try to solve the problem at hand. Solving problems can be a nice thing to do, but first you need to acknowledge your partner's feelings about the situation. If you dismiss those feelings, he or she probably won't be receptive to whatever solutions you bring forth.

The final barrier to connecting more deeply with your partner is simple *distraction*. Over the course of a single day in America, the average person consults a smartphone an average of 143 times and watches almost four and a half hours of TV. Amazingly, 20 percent of people regularly look at their smartphones during sex! That's a lot of distraction. We all need to be entertained once in a while, but if your media consumption, drugs, or other distractions keep you from connecting with your mate, you've got a problem. Overcoming distractions is one more reason why deliberate communication exercises can be so helpful in removing the various obstacles to deeper connection.

Mahatma Gandhi once said: "I have only three enemies. My favorite enemy, the one most easily influenced for the better, is the British Empire. My second enemy, the Indian people, are far more difficult. But my most formidable opponent is a man named Mohandas K. Gandhi. With him, I seem to have very little influence." Gandhi clearly understood how hard it is to change our behavior. It's easy to tell our partners that they need to change. The real question is: "Are *we* willing to change?"

Learning anything new is usually difficult. But I've learned that, with the right information, the right tools, and a clear goal, change is possible. In fact, miracles are possible.

Simple and Easy Practice

The next time you're experiencing a nice connection with your partner, ask about his or her view of how you both handle stress as a couple. You can simply ask: "What have you noticed about how you and I relate when we're stressed? What patterns do we typically fall into?" Listen and affirm what your mate says. Being aware of a pattern or problem is the biggest step you can take to overcoming it. Once you've heard your partner's perspective, you can offer your own insights. You may even offer a strategy or two from this book. Talking about your "stress patterns" is a great way to step out of them. If you can bring humor to such a conversation, you get major bonus points. You may find that the next time you're both stressed, remembering your typical patterns can prevent you from diving deeply into them.

CHAPTER 2

The Power of Desire

It can be extremely useful to look at yourself and your partner in terms of what you each truly desire or value in an intimate relationship. To the extent that you can satisfy your partner's strongest desires, he or she will be very happy with you. To the extent that your partner can satisfy your deepest desires, you'll be very happy with your partner. Pretty simple.

Knowing what you and your partner most value is the first step to having those desires satisfied. Once these desires are brought to light, you can more easily steer your communication and behavior toward meeting each other's needs. Unfortunately, most people don't have a clue as to what they or their partners really want. No one ever comes right out on a first date and says: "I'm really looking for safety and security. Is that something you would be good at giving me and enjoy providing?"

In chapter 1, we learned that everybody is really looking for care, understanding, and empathy—CUE. This is true for all of us. It's in our biological makeup. Yet people want other things as well, and we all value them differently. At the end of this chapter, I give a list of what I call the Fifty Universal Desires, which consists of words that describe things people want in their intimate relationships. Let's see how one couple responded when asked to identify desires from this list.

Sarah and Brian entered my office as a last-ditch effort to avoid divorce. Sarah hit me with a list of complaints about Brian, expecting that I would somehow set him straight. Brian just sat there with his arms folded against his chest, occasionally giving me an eye roll that silently said to me: "This is the crap I have to deal with." Somewhere around Sarah's tenth criticism of her husband, I asked her a question that stopped her in her tracks. The question was: "If Brian changed in all the ways you wanted, what would you have that you don't have now?"

At first, Sarah couldn't answer the question. I explained to her that you can't hit a target if you don't know what the target is. Then I showed her the list of Fifty Universal Desires and asked her to circle five words on the list that struck her as something she deep-down really wanted in her marriage. Suddenly, the anger drained from her face. Sarah started circling her five words: safety, affection, companionship, intimacy, and belonging. I noticed tears in her eyes as she reflected on her chosen words. I asked her what she was feeling and she responded: "This is all I've ever wanted, and I see I'm not getting any of it."

It was true that Sarah's desires were not being met, but I explained to her that it didn't have to stay that way. Her acknowledgment of her actual desires was an important first step in helping her get what she really wanted. Once she knew precisely what she really wanted, I asked her: "How can you communicate or behave in a way that makes the fulfillment of your desires more likely?" It's an important question to consider. After all, criticizing your partner probably won't lead to things like safety, affection, or belonging. In fact, Sarah did not *know* how to communicate in a way that could lead to these things.

When I asked Barry what five words he would choose from the list, he circled ease, independence, pleasure, respect, and discovery. It became immediately apparent that Barry and Sarah wanted very different things. That's okay. You don't have to want exactly the same things in order to have a successful relationship. We'll look more at this later in the chapter.

Just Like Me

A major obstacle to meeting our partners' desires can be the judgments we make about how they have gone about satisfying their needs in the past. When we judge our partners, we express a belief that they shouldn't be the way they are. I confess that sometimes I get judgmental about my wife's behavior. Occasionally, I see that her strategy for satisfying her desires is ineffective or even opposed to her ultimate goal. Then I fall into feelings of self-righteousness and superiority. My friend and fellow author Arjuna Ardagh (*ArjunaArdagh.com*) taught me to say three magical words at such times to put a quick halt to my judgments. Those three magical words are: "Just like me."

The words "just like me" are a very effective antidote to self-righteous and judgmental thinking. After all, *I* often behave in ways that don't lead to the intimacy I desire, so when I see this behavior in others, it invokes a feeling of compassion. We're all human, and we all let our past conditioning influence our actions in detrimental ways from time to time. When you see something you don't like in your mate and you want to let go of your judgments quickly, try thinking the words "just like me," and notice how it makes you feel. For me, it often brings up a feeling of compassion—or, at the very least, it helps me to let go of my judgments quickly.

Another way to avoid making judgments is to see your partner as simply trying to satisfy his or her deep-seated desires. After all, that's what human beings do—they try to satisfy their innermost desires. We are biologically programmed to do so. Desires are not bad. They motivate us to take action. The problem is that the ways in which people go about fulfilling their desires can sometimes cause suffering. People often use strategies that are ineffective or totally counterproductive. But once you're clear on what you and your partner really want, you can work toward achieving it in productive ways. When you work to satisfy each other's true desires, love will flow between you.

Positive Intention

One of my favorite ways to let go of my judgments is to tune into my wife's "positive intention." A positive intention is the *ultimate* positive reason your partner is pursuing a certain behavior. For example, if your partner complains a lot, you probably don't like that behavior. However, you can tune into the positive intention motivating it. The positive reason someone complains may be a desire for more comfort or pleasure or to feel better. Those are all fine things to want. The problem is that your partner's strategy for obtaining them may be counterproductive in the long term. Trying to figure out what your partner ultimately wants from his or her "irritating" actions can be a major step in establishing empathy.

When couples in my office are critical of each other, I often ask them: "What do you think is the positive intention of your partner's behavior?" This question can quickly put a stop to their blaming. Try it for yourself right now. Think of a behavior your partner does that you don't like. Stop reading for a moment and really do this. Now ask yourself: "What could the positive intention be behind that behavior?" If you're having trouble, look at the list of Universal Desires at the end of this chapter and see what jumps out at you. If you can imagine your partner's positive intention, it will help you let go of judgment and allow you to be more accepting. Such acceptance is often the first step to helping your partner find a more effective method for achieving what he or she really wants.

While judging your partner is never helpful, mistrust is even more hurtful to an intimate relationship. When you continually question your partner's motivations or intent, you destroy any chance of trust developing in your relationship. Trust and faith are the bedrock of a strong partnership. Without it, couples don't have what it takes to weather the inevitable storms most relationships face.

Kevin and Jen were dealing with intense jealousy issues. Whenever Kevin mentioned female friends in his life, Jen got very jealous and upset. After a while, Kevin was hesitant to say *anything* about his interactions with his female friends. This led Jen to accuse him of being dishonest and sneaky. So I asked Jen: "What could Kevin's positive intention be for not ever talking about his interactions with women?" A light seemed to go on in her head. She realized he was just trying to feel safety and ease. Coincidently, these were the same desires *she* was longing for. Once she saw that Kevin was just trying to feel safe and avoid conflict by not talking about his female friends, it softened Jen's heart. Soon, she found herself feeling compassion for Kevin—rather than distrust and anger.

Understanding your partner's positive intention gives you very important and powerful information. It will inevitably help you to feel more accepting. In any relationship, full acceptance is like a magical elixir. We all crave acceptance and love. When people feel accepted, they feel safe to be themselves—rather than afraid, hesitant, or defensive. This inevitably increases *your* level of ease and intimacy as well. In addition, knowing your partner's positive intention can help open up the lines of communication between you. For example, if you know that your partner's complaints are really motivated by a desire to feel more security, you can ask: "What would help you to feel even more secure in our relationship?" This is likely to be much more helpful than asking: "Why do you complain all the time?"

Five Simple Questions

When couples come into my office with a specific problem, I often guide them through a process to help them quickly get to the bottom of it. The "process" consists of asking five simple questions that I learned from Scott Catamas, who offers free online videos on his website *LoveCoachAcademy.com*. These five questions are incredibly effective at helping couples go from anger and blame to compassion and connection.

1. What stories am I telling myself about this situation?
2. What do I really want?
3. What am I feeling?
4. What do I imagine my partner is thinking, wanting, and feeling?
5. How can I listen and express myself in a way that shows my partner my care, understanding, and empathy?

Let's go through each of these questions to see why they are so effective and exactly how to use them.

- *What stories am I telling myself about this situation?* Whenever we face a challenge with our partners, we create a story about it. Usually the stories are ones of blame, betrayal, or victimhood. As we repeat these stories in our heads, we not only affirm how right we are, but we also get worked up into a tizzy. However, no matter how "good" our stories are, there's always another side to reality. Just realizing that we're telling ourselves a story—rather than an impartial description of reality—can help us to gain some perspective. Since we tend to "play" the same loop over and over in our heads, after a while we can come to recognize our most damaging stories and not get so worked up about them.

- *What do I really want?* This question takes us back to the idea that the best way to hit a target is to know precisely where or what the target is. The list of Universal Desires at the end of this chapter can help you define what you're really longing for.

- *What am I feeling?* Knowing your true feelings is important because it can help indicate what story you're really telling yourself, as well as how you're reacting to it. In addition, when you realize you're stuck in a feeling you don't like, it can help motivate you to try a different approach to getting what you most desire.

- *What do I imagine my partner is thinking, wanting, and feeling?* This question is key if you want to overcome a problem and reconnect with your partner. Normally, when a difficult issue arises, we lose touch with what our partners' are experiencing. Of course, they sense this and are put off by our lack of care, understanding, and empathy (CUE). However, when we enter our partners' world and feel the difficulty they're having, they sense it. In fact, it can be a game changer. Once you begin to care, understand, and empathize with how your partner feels, connection is quickly restored and the problem at hand often dissolves on its own.

- *How can I listen and express myself in a way that shows my partner my care, understanding, and empathy?* As you become more skilled at the communication methods in this book, your answer to this question will become more precise. However, just asking the question will help point you in the right direction.

Juan and Camila came into my office and began with: "We only have money for one session. Can you help us? We're desperate." I said I'd do my best. They told me that Juan had been laid off from his job and that he and Camila were arguing a lot now that both of them were home. I used the five questions to get to the heart of the problem quickly:

Me: Camila, what stories are you telling yourself about this situation?

Camila: I'm telling myself that we're going to end up homeless because we have no money and Juan is too lazy to look for a job. I'm telling myself that I won't be able to be home for my kids anymore and that they'll get into trouble. I'm telling myself that I'm going to be a single mom with no job and no money.

Me: With stories like that, I can understand why you're so upset. Can you be absolutely sure those stories are true—that they will come to pass?

Camila: No. Now that I said them out loud, I realize they're a bit dramatic.

Me: That's a good insight. Sometimes the stories we create are just there to scare us. Camila, what are you really wanting? Look at this list of Universal Desires and tell me what are three or four things that really call out to you?

Camila: I want security, I want nurturing, respect, and belonging.

I told Camila that those are all wonderful things to want. But, for better or worse, often the best way to get these things is to *give* them to your partner. What goes around comes around. Then I asked her what some of the feelings were that she had been struggling with lately.

Camila: I've been feeling a lot of anger.

Me: Anger often covers up other feelings that feel more vulnerable. Would you say that underneath your anger is more of a sense of hurt, or sadness, or perhaps fear?

Camila: Fear. I'm afraid of being homeless, of being a single mom with no money and no job.

I told her I could understand how she would feel afraid of that scenario and then moved on to the next question. I asked her to imagine what Juan was thinking, feeling, and needing in their current situation.

Camila: I don't really know. I guess maybe he's thinking that he failed me and the kids. Maybe he's feeling hopeless or depressed. I don't really know what he needs.

Me: Well, which of these five things do you think he needs from you at this point: criticism, resentment, support, tenderness, or disappointment?

Camila: Support and tenderness.

Me: So it sounds as if you *do* know what he needs.

Then I moved on to the last question. I asked her to consider how she could listen and express herself in a way that showed Juan she cared, understood, and empathized?

Camila: I guess I can tell him I believe in him and that we're in this together. I can stop telling him he's lazy and ask him if there's anything I can do to support him.

Me: Have you been doing those things?

Camila: No.

I pointed out that by adopting the suggestions she came up with, she could make Juan feel her support. I said that changing her behavior would encourage him to do whatever it took to have things work out for their family. She agreed to give it a try.

By the time Camila and Juan walked out of the session, they were clearly on the same team again. These five questions helped them discern which direction they needed to travel. I've seen this work with dozens of couples, and it only takes a couple of minutes. You don't even need your partner there to go through the questions. You can do it completely on your own. A common reaction I hear when people ask themselves these five questions is: "I was surprised at how much my *partner* changed while I was asking *myself* these questions!" Frankly, our partners are our mirrors. As *our* attitudes change, our partners simply reflect the changes we make in ourselves.

Simple and Easy Practice

Look at the list of Fifty Universal Desires below and circle the four or five that strike you as being the most important to you. Then, when the time feels right, ask your partner: "What are the things you most want from me in our relationship?" If the list of Universal Desires is nearby, you can share it. Take careful note of what your partner says. The more you can satisfy what is most important to your mate, the happier he or she will be with you.

Another practice that can be extremely helpful is to figure out what you truly desire when you're upset. This information is not usually clear to us. We tend to get caught up in thinking that we simply want our partners to be different from what they are. But you can get to the root of what you're *really* after by asking yourself this simple question: "If my partner changed in the ways I wanted, what would I have more of that I feel I don't have now?" Then, go down the list of Fifty Universal Desires and identify what you're really wanting. For example, if you have a hard time with your partner's temper, you may really be wanting more safety, or acceptance, or ease. If you ask yourself this question whenever you have a complaint about your partner, it will become increasingly clear what you truly desire and value in your partnership.

Fifty Universal Desires

Safety	Security
Trust	Ease
Independence	Spontaneity
Humor	Joy
Pleasure	Affection
Closeness	Companionship
Intimacy	Love
Nurturing	Sexual expression
Tenderness	Acceptance
Care	Compassion
Consideration	Empathy
Kindness	Understanding
Respect	Belonging
Cooperation	Equality, fairness
Partnership	Authenticity
Creativity	Integrity
Honesty	Self-care
Self-realization	Learning
Discovery	Challenge
Contribution	Exploration
Purpose	Beauty
Support	Faith
Presence	Inspiration
Mutual recognition	Peace of mind
Transcendence	Gratitude

CHAPTER 3

Keys to Connection

As we saw in chapter 2, the most important key to a better connection with people is to understand their unique needs and desires. However, there are several other factors involved in creating successful communication. For instance, if you say the right words, but with the wrong attitude, you will not be successful. Nonverbal behavior—the tone of your voice and your body language—can drown out your words if you're not careful. If you speak words of appreciation to your partner with a tone of sarcasm in your voice, your mate will not feel loved but rather belittled and distrustful. On the other hand, if you display the right tone and attitude in your communication, the exact words you use will not be all that important. We'll talk more about nonverbal communication in chapter 19.

There are five key attitudes that are important and helpful in establishing effective and constructive communication: curiosity, generosity, vulnerability, gratitude, and responsibility. You do not need to display all five of these, however, to have your communication go well. In fact, simply displaying any *one* of them will usually be enough to turn a difficult communication around. Most people find that they are already pretty good at one or more of these attitudes and hopelessly bad at some of the others. Start by making better use of the one attitude you find easiest to embrace. For example, I am naturally a curious person, so when possible, I lead with curiosity. I ask questions. I wonder about why people say certain things. I am truly interested in their experiences. My mate and my friends appreciate this sincere curiosity. That helps them cut me some slack when they see that my ability to be vulnerable is not so great.

Curiosity

Curiosity is the recognition that you don't know something but that you'd like to know it. When your mate understands that you're truly curious about what he or she thinks or feels, it is enlivening. Think back to when you knew someone was really interested in something about you or something you did. It likely felt very validating. Besides helping your mate to feel better, the answers you receive to your questions can be very helpful in your relationship.

An important aspect of being curious is the ability to ask good questions. However, in reality, not all questions are motivated by curiosity. Take, for example, the question: "Why did you come home late again?" This could be asked from true curiosity, or it could be a subtle form of accusation. Attorneys ask people in courtrooms many questions, but none of those questions come from actual curiosity. In the same way, I often see couples ask each other questions when their motivation is really to blame or accuse.

Michael and Melinda came to see me because they were fighting too much. I talked to them about the value of curiosity and asking good questions. Michael said he'd give it a try. His first question to his wife was: "Why don't you appreciate anything I do for you?" Before Melinda could respond (or hit Michael over the head), I interrupted. I explained that questions like this come off as statements of blame—not of curiosity.

Michael tried again. His next question was: "Why are you upset all the time?" He clearly spoke with resentment. Strike two. I explained that most questions grounded in sincere curiosity are very specific, while general questions like the ones he was asking tended to hide words of denigration or judgment.

With one strike left, Michael said: "What is something I could do that you would really appreciate?" Home run. Michael really didn't know the answer to this question, so it was a true question coming from curiosity. Melinda was happy to answer his sincere inquiry.

When our partners feel that we really are curious and want to know something, it softens them. To set the stage correctly, I often preface my questions with a qualifier like: "I'm confused about something, and I'm wondering if you can help me understand it better." Then I ask my question. The response is always good. When your mate senses you truly *are* curious, it sets the stage for the establishment of care, understanding, and empathy.

Perhaps the biggest obstacle to curiosity is thinking you already know the answer. Don't ever assume you know a person or situation completely. There's always something new to learn.

Generosity

In communication, generosity means leading with the heart. It means showing kindness, appreciation, and acknowledgment. The good news is that these traits are lacking in most people's communications. I call that good news because, if you learn to include them regularly in *your* communication, you will stand out like a saint.

Dr. John Gottman is a famous marriage researcher and author of the bestseller, *The Seven Principles for Making Marriage Work*. In his studies, he has found that one of the best predictors of a happy marriage is the ratio of positive to negative comments. If couples say five positive things to their partners for every negative comment they make, they invariably rate their marriage as very happy. However, if there are more negative comments than positive ones, they rate their marriage as unhappy. Pretty simple. Of course, it's not hard to make nice comments; it just takes a willingness to ask yourself: "What is something I have liked or appreciated about my partner recently?" Then say it.

Don't wait until you like everything about your partner before you express your approval. That may never happen. You need only find one specific thing you like in order to express appreciation. Just find one thing you genuinely *do* appreciate and let your partner know about it. The more you make expressing appreciation and acknowledgment a habit, the more generosity you'll bring to your relationship. True generosity almost always generates a reciprocal response, just as meanness leads to more nastiness. If you find that you and your partner are caught in a nastiness spell, an attitude of generosity can often break the cycle.

In my counseling practice, I often hear how small acts of kindness—offering your mate a shoulder massage or cooking a favorite meal—are what "tip" the relationship back to love and harmony. The opposite is also true. Small acts of inconsideration can wreak havoc in a relationship. Since acts of kindness feel good (for both partners) and have a deep healing effect, their power should not be overlooked. Unfortunately, acts of kindness and generosity are rare in our world of constant busyness and distraction. Yet, if you are habitually generous with your words and deeds, you may be amazed at how people—including your partner—respond.

Another way of delineating what generosity looks like in communication is to describe what it is *not*. Katrina Vaillancourt (*LoveSmartCards.com*) has made a list of ten common ways couples respond to each other that are not generous. Below is a list of these ungenerous responses, as well as examples of what they sound like in relationships:

1. *Judging:* criticizing your mate's point of view ("Well, I see how you treat the kids, and I can understand why they don't want to spend more time around you.")

2. *Blaming:* placing your partner in the wrong ("We're not having sex more often because you're always too tired.")

3. *Shaming:* implying your partner is essentially a bad person ("If you were a more caring person, we wouldn't be having these problems.")

4. *Comparing:* contrasting your partner's behavior with someone who demonstrates preferential behavior ("You need to be more like Cheryl. She doesn't get upset as easily as you do.")

5. *Denying:* invalidating your partner's experience of reality ("Don't be silly. There's really nothing to worry about here.")

6. *Colluding:* agreeing with your partner's disempowerng complaints ("Your friends really are mean and nasty a lot of the time.")

7. *Advising or preaching:* providing feedback or advice to a partner who is not asking for it. ("You really need to eat better so you're not sick so often.")

8. *Interrogating:* using questions to blame your partner and/or change their behavior ("Do you think your frequent eating of ice cream and cookies is why you have gained so much weight?")

9. *Psychoanalyzing:* telling your partner what their "true" motives are ("You get upset at the kids because you need to be in control all the time.")

10. *Dismissing:* minimizing your partner's reality ("It can't be that bad at work. Most of the time your boss is a nice guy.")

As you can see, there are many and varied ways to display a lack of generosity in your communication. You may even think such responses are justified or helpful, but the truth is that they tend to create distance rather than intimacy. By recognizing all the ways couples fail to be generous with each other, you have a better chance of hitting the target of true empathy and kindness with your own partner.

Vulnerability

Brené Brown is a well-known self-help author and social psychology researcher. In books like *Daring Greatly*, she argues eloquently that true vulnerability can actually be very powerful. The problem is that, in our culture, we're taught that vulnerability is weakness. As a man, it has not always been easy for me to share my vulnerable feelings and thoughts. I was taught to be strong. But over time, I noticed that my wife loved me more when I was able to convey my vulnerability. Think back to what *you* appreciate in your partner. Do you appreciate it most when he or she is full of assurance, self-righteousness, and bluster? Or do you prefer it when your mate is truthful, authentic, and vulnerable? Most people prefer vulnerability over bluster.

When I was in my twenties, I conducted a one-month experiment in extreme vulnerability. I decided to travel across the country with zero money. To get around, I hitchhiked. When hungry, I asked people for food or for money to buy food. Sometimes, I went into a town and just knocked on random doors. When someone answered, I said something like: "Hi, my name is Jonathan. I'm trying to live off other people's generosity for a month as a way of experiencing vulnerability and surrender. I'm a bit hungry and cold, so anything you can offer will be greatly appreciated."

You're probably guessing not that many people offered to help me out. Yet, in a month of asking for help, over 90 percent of the people I approached offered me some kind of assistance. One elderly gentleman even offered to drive me to my next destination—which was more than sixty miles away. From this experience, I learned that true vulnerability brings out the best in others. A soft open heart in one person arouses a similar reaction in another. The same is true in relationships. When one person taps into authentic vulnerability, it leads to a shared heart space.

Gratitude

Gratitude for your partner is like a powerful elixir. Just a little can go a long way toward cementing your bond. When you live with someone day after day, however, it's easy to take that person for granted. That's why I was intrigued when a friend told me he'd met a guru in India who gave him a mantra for feeling gratitude toward his wife. Unfortunately, he wouldn't tell me what the mantra was. He said I had to go to India and get it directly from the guru. I really wanted to know what this technique was, so I booked a flight to India and traveled by rickshaw for three hours to the guru's ashram. After waiting in line for four hours, I finally got a chance to ask this holy man about his magical mantra for feeling more gratitude in marriage.

The guru looked me over and said: "Yes, my mantra is the most powerful mantra on Earth." He told me to come close, so I leaned in next to him. He put his mouth close to my ear and whispered: "Whenever possible, repeat the following words in your head. . . " By now, I was so excited that I literally stopped breathing so I would be sure to hear the magical words correctly. After a brief pause, the guru finally said: "The mantra I give you are the words, '*Thank you*.'"

I was stunned. At first, I thought he was joking, but as I looked up at him, he wasn't smiling. I stared at him for a moment and then practically shouted: "Thank you! I traveled eighteen thousand miles to hear the words 'thank you'? *That's it?*"

The guru said: "No, 'That's it?' is the mantra you *have* been using and *that* mantra makes you feel as if you never have enough. My mantra is 'Thank you,' not 'That's it?' Your mantra will take you *nowhere*. But 'Thank you' will quiet your mind and open your heart. But you must say it many, many times a day for each person in your life, and you must say it from your heart. So when you see your wonderful partner in the morning, say to yourself, 'Thank you.' When you see your child or your pet, say 'Thank you' in your heart. Soon you will feel overwhelming gratitude."

Well, I was pretty angry and disappointed, but, having traveled all that distance, I figured I would try out the "mantra." When I got back to my hotel, I Skyped with my wife. As I saw her beautiful face on the screen, internally I said to myself: "Thank you." I realized how lucky we were to be able to talk to each other—for free—across the planet. Another "thank you." When my wife said that she and our dogs were doing well, I said another "thank you" from my heart. To my astonishment, I soon had tears of gratitude dripping from my eyes. This guru's simple mantra actually worked!

Try it for yourself. When you see your partner throughout the day, say a silent "thank you" from your heart and see what magic results from your feelings of gratitude. Even when we don't say it out loud, our partners can pick up on whether we feel gratitude toward them or not. Just think of one specific thing for which you're grateful. As you cultivate an attitude of gratitude in your relationship, you'll find that more love and less conflict will follow.

Responsibility

Last, but not least, is the attitude of responsibility. Earlier, I mentioned that blame or denigration is the typical way in which couples in crisis relate to each other. Unfortunately, blame never gets us anywhere. After we tell our partners how idiotic and wrong they've been, they *never* suddenly realize how right we actually are. Our secret fantasy is that they will apologize when we tell them about their annoying misdeeds. However, if you look at how often blame, complaint, and denigration work, you'll see that it's—well, never. Zero. Zip. Zilch. It never works the way we hope it will.

Taking responsibility is not easy. In a relationship, it requires a willingness to be brutally honest with yourself. Our egos never like to admit that we made a mistake or that we hurt someone else. Because we all know that taking responsibility is difficult, when we hear someone do it, it has an enormous impact. If you've ever had your partner take responsibility for something that upset you, you probably noticed how it immediately calmed you down. If you were angry or hurt, those feelings may have quickly dissipated. When our partners take responsibility, it promptly opens the door to forgiveness, honest communication, and intimacy. Because taking responsibility is so powerful, it's important to learn how to do it more frequently and effectively.

At its most basic level, taking responsibility involves answering a specific question: "How has my behavior (specifically) contributed to the problems we are now dealing with?" If you can answer that question in the midst of a heated exchange with your partner, two things will likely happen. First, the argument will instantly end as your partner's heart softens. Second, your partner will be astonished at your act of courage.

In my private practice, I notice that people are often quite clear about how their partners are to blame for the difficulties at hand but clueless as to how *they* are responsible. When I ask partners how their behavior may have contributed to the problems they're now dealing with, I mostly get blank stares—as if their IQs suddenly dropped by about eighty points. With practice, however, people can learn to answer that question. As with any other skill, taking responsibility gets easier with practice, a good method, and a sincere desire to improve. It's one of the most powerful ways not only to end an argument but also to deepen and soften the connection with your mate immediately.

Simple and Easy Practice

Choose one specific attitude to focus on with your partner for a week—or even for a day. Really attempt to practice that attitude to the best of your ability as often as possible. Notice at the end of this time how it has affected your relationship. If you like the effect, keep it going. Here are some simple and easy things you can try for each of the five attitudes:

- *Curiosity:* Ask your partner questions about his or her day, or feelings, or hopes in life. Use some of the questions given in this book to get to know your partner more deeply and intimately.

- *Generosity:* Each day, tell your partner something you appreciate about him or her. Alternately, do small acts of kindness—like buying a little gift or giving a shoulder massage.

- *Vulnerability:* Reveal vulnerable feelings to your partner—an expression of love, gratitude, sadness, fear, or inadequacy. Tell your partner something you regret or something you wish you could do better in your relationship.

- *Gratitude:* Express a sincere "thank you" (from your heart) for any act of kindness your partner does. Tell him or her exactly what you are very grateful for in your relationship.

- *Responsibility:* Think of an issue or tension you have in your relationship. Then ask yourself: "How has my behavior (specifically) contributed to the problem we are now dealing with?" At an appropriate time, reveal your answer to your partner.

CHAPTER 4

Vive la Différence!

When it comes to communication, everyone has a slightly different style. Sometimes our way of communicating can be so different from our partners' approach that it can feel as if we're talking to an alien. Books like *Men Are from Mars, Women Are from Venus* popularized the notion that men and women have very different needs and communication patterns. But the truth is a bit more complicated than that. Therefore, it can be helpful to understand how to communicate with anyone with a style different from your own—regardless of gender.

To keep things simple, I like to sort communication styles into two broad categories. One consists of people who tend to be very *direct* in their communication. These people always have a goal in mind when they communicate. Rather than providing details about their day, they say what they want and try to direct their conversations to a specific result. If married to a person with this style, you may hear words like: "What time is the party on Wednesday?" or "Can you walk the dog tomorrow morning?" Their communication tends to be focused, task-oriented, and to the point.

At the other end of the spectrum are those who communicate in an *indirect* manner. People who speak in this way don't have a clear goal in mind when they communicate. Instead, when talking with others about almost anything, they establish a connection first. They prioritize their empathic connection with others as the most important thing, rather than trying to achieve a result. If married to a person with this style, you may hear them say things like: "How was your day?" or "Did you notice that the trees are blooming?" or "It is really wonderful weather, isn't it?" Indirect communicators are not necessarily trying to get information from their questions and statements. What they really value is emotional connection.

In my counseling practice, I inevitably see couples who lie on opposite ends of the direct/indirect communication spectrum. When partners have opposite ways of relating and communicating, it can drive them crazy. Each couple establishes its own unique pattern. It can even occur that partners who communicate directly at work may tend to communicate indirectly in their private relationships. Ultimately, neither style is better than the other. They both have their uses. But if your partner tends toward one end of the spectrum and you the other, it is important that you learn to respect and "speak" your partner's preferred "language."

There are good reasons why people learn and adopt a certain style of communication. First, there's genetics. In the distant past, men were trained to be hunters. In such a world, being empathic or indirect was not a helpful survival strategy. The culture we're raised in also plays a part in determining our communication pattern. For example, the Japanese are known for being incredibly polite and formal, whereas Americans are known for their informality.

Finally, perhaps the biggest impact on our communication style comes from our unique family environment. If your parents were loud and quick to anger, then you're more likely to be just like them—or the opposite of them. If your brother or sister bullied you, then there's a good chance that you grew up to be that way yourself. Understanding the reasons why your partner may communicate in a style different from your own can make it easier to feel less judgmental. Don't disparage your partner for how he or she communicates. Instead, seek to better understand your mate's unique style.

Besides different communication styles, couples also have different ways of working through their feelings and problems. Some people like to work through problems and feelings indirectly— perhaps by doing something physical or distracting. Going to the gym, working on the computer, or having some time alone helps them get over what was bothering them. On the other hand, people with a more direct way of working through feelings and problems use a completely different approach. When under stress, they are likely to want to connect immediately with their partners and talk about their feelings. If their partners suggest that they shouldn't worry so much—or that they should just go to the gym—the result may not be pretty. In these cases, it's important to realize that what works for you when you are under stress may be exactly the opposite of what works for your partner.

Even if your partner and you have totally different styles of communicating, understanding and care can help bridge the gap. I learned this lesson with my dog. I love my dog very much. We have a great relationship—filled with love, joy, and very few communication problems. One reason for this is that I fully understand that her way of communicating and her desires are very different from my own. For instance, she likes to chase squirrels. Well, chasing squirrels is not my thing—but I let her do it because it's important to her. After all, she and I are different animals. Likewise, if you and your partner are different "animals," don't focus on trying to make your mate be like you. In fact, that would be impossible. Instead, focus on understanding what's important to your mate and learn to support him or her as best you can.

Here's an example from my own relationship. My wife understands that I have limited capacity for talking about feelings. When she comes home from work, she likes to talk about her day and her feelings. Well, talking about my day after work is not my thing. I prefer to watch TV or have a quick conversation about what needs to get done around the house. But I find that, when I listen to what my wife has to say about her day, she inevitably feels more loving toward me and rewards me with more physical affection. I could tell my wife that rambling on about her day and her feelings is a waste of time, but that's like telling my dog she shouldn't chase squirrels. It simply won't work.

Understanding someone's preferred communication style can also help you navigate better when the road gets bumpy. Those who are direct in how they like to handle their feelings need time to vent with little or no response. Someone just being there, not trying to fix anything, and listening empathically is what a direct-feeling partner craves. Conversely, partners who handle feelings and problems indirectly need time to do whatever helps them to work through issues. Constant probing and a desire for a quick resolution will only serve to upset them more.

When Sean and Tova walked into my office, I could tell they were on opposite sides of the direct/indirect continuum for handling feelings. Sean resented Tova's frequent questions—sometimes as simple as: "How are you feeling?" Conversely, Tova was upset that Sean seemed bored and avoided eye contact whenever she talked about her feelings. Tova got livid when Sean quickly ran out of patience and blurted out: "You're making a big deal out of nothing." They had each spent years trying to convince the other that their own way of handling feelings was superior. Neither had been convinced. I suggested that they accept each other's different communication patterns and learn to give each other what they craved.

With my coaching, Sean eventually learned to avoid belittling Tova's feelings or giving her advice when she talked about her day. If he was too stressed or too tired to listen to her, he simply asked for some time alone before connecting with her. For her part, Tova stopped asking daily questions about Sean's feelings. Instead, they agreed he'd talk about his feelings once a week during a structured communication exercise. Free from the burden of trying to change each other, Sean and Tova found they had a lot more time simply to enjoy each other.

Google has created a pretty good translation algorithm that can translate English into dozens of other languages in real time. It's a great tool. However, what we really need is an algorithm that can translate communication styles. Alas, such an algorithm does not exist (yet), so we have to learn how to adapt to our partners' different styles for ourselves. Understanding the ways in which our partners interpret our speech, or learning how best to talk in a way they can relate to, can be complicated. That's one reason why the communication exercises offered in this book can be so useful. They act as a temporary "translation tool." Each method provides a structure that makes good communication more likely. When couples use a communication exercise, they often feel as if they are finally speaking the same language.

The Great Divide

About fifty years ago, the rules for a happy partnership started going through a radical change. Women began entering the workforce in greater numbers and could take care of themselves financially. This shift left men with less clarity as to their own purpose and left women wanting men to be more than just providers. While this shift was necessary and ultimately for the good, it created an emotional rift between many men and women. The divorce rate skyrocketed, and a lot of couples experienced problems that were the result of the cultural changes taking place.

As women began working outside the home more, they wanted to have their emotional—rather than financial—needs met by their mates. As men became more focused on meeting their mate's emotional needs, they sometimes felt a loss of their sense of purpose and manhood. Over time, many women became more "masculine" in their energy, as they took on more earning power and men took on more caregiving roles. According to David Deida, author of *The Way of the Superior Man*, this led to less sexual energy between men and women. After all, sexual energy is about the union of opposites. That's why many modern couples feel less passion in their relationships than in previous decades. Many men and women have, to some extent, met in the middle, with the result that many couples end up being more like friends than passionate partners.

When two people have very different ways of dealing with feelings, the upside can be that there is actually more "polarity" between them. Increased polarity, like the positive and negative charges in a battery, can lead to more (sexual) energy. When couples have *similar* styles of communication and dealing with feelings, this can create a lack of polarity—and thus less passion. In a world in which sexual roles and energy are often less distinct than they were fifty years ago, couples can often find themselves with less polarity and less passion than they desire.

There are no quick fixes for this common problem in long-term relationships. However, Deida offers some interesting ideas about how to create more polarity in any relationship. He suggests that, for women to create more polarity with their male partners, they focus on being more "feminine," cultivating things like beauty, nurturing, creativity, and dance. He maintains that men are most attracted to women who can fully display their feminine energy.

This includes vulnerability, innocence, playfulness, sensuality, and beauty. Since many men lack these traits, any woman who displays them is more likely to create polarity with a male partner. On the other hand, Deida claims, a man can often create more polarity with a woman by displaying more "masculine" energy and traits. This can include traits like being steadfast, resolute, and not frightened by a woman's emotions. Although his generalizations don't apply to all couples, there are many who have found that his ideas have merit.

Michelle and Matthew entered my office with the complaint that they had become more like roommates than husband and wife. Their sex life had deteriorated to the point of making love less than once every other month. They both worked stressful jobs, and it was clear they had lost all their passion for each other. I proposed that they try an experiment. I recommended that, for one month, Matthew focus on acting and being as "masculine" as possible, while Michelle concentrate on being as "feminine" as possible. We all agreed that it would be interesting to see what effect this would have on their relationship.

To make their task easier, I gave Matthew and Michelle some specific things they each could do. I suggested that Matthew could better feel his masculine energy by increasing his physical activity, spending time reconnecting with male friends, or doing something adventurous. For Michelle, I suggested she devote time to self-care, creative endeavors, or connecting with loved ones. The hope was that, as they mindfully connected with their primal energy, they would rekindle the flame of their relationship.

Along with this emphasis on being more masculine or feminine, I also asked Matthew and Michelle to alter how they spoke to each other for the month-long experiment. I asked Matthew, who had become somewhat indirect in his communication style, to become more direct and goal-oriented. I suggested that he directly express when he felt like making love and tell his wife when he felt she was looking especially attractive to him. I asked Michelle, whose job had swayed her toward being a direct communicator, to talk more about her feelings. By doing this, I hoped they would create more polarity between them, and hopefully spark some extra sexual energy.

The results of this experiment were actually quite remarkable. While they admitted that they had to force themselves to "play" their respective roles for the first few days, soon their spark reignited and their passion expanded. With big smiles, they told me that they had decided to keep the experiment going after the month ended.

Simple and Easy Practice

Whether you tend toward being a direct or indirect communicator, try the other approach for a day. If you have an inclination to get quickly to the point, talk about your feelings instead. If you already talk easily about your feelings, pretend you're a CEO barking out demands and requests. Notice how it feels to speak this slightly "foreign" language. By doing this, you may find you have a better understanding of your partner, or you may find it creates more sexual polarity between the two of you.

There's a well-known adage that claims: "What you appreciate appreciates." In relationships, this means that, if your partner communicates or behaves in a way that is new and you like it, appreciate it immediately. Don't wait to praise until your mate can express his or her feelings perfectly or communicate exactly in the way you would like. Appreciating any small effort or change you notice will encourage your partner to keep moving in that direction.

CHAPTER 5

Communication Workout

We've covered many of the fundamentals of a good relationship so far. I wish that were enough. Unfortunately, it isn't. I hate to be the bearer of bad news, but the next time you and your partner have a difficult time, you'll likely forget everything you just learned. That's just the way it is. The good news is that I have a remedy for this. It's called a "communication workout." The exercises that make up this workout make good communication possible even when you'd rather tear your partner apart. They provide a structure that assures success—even if you can't remember any of the helpful theory and tips provided in the previous chapters.

The analogy of a physical workout is useful here. When you go to the gym, you don't complain about the heaviness of the weights or the difficulty you may have lifting them. After all, that difficulty is the key ingredient in your becoming stronger. In a similar way, the difficulty you have in a relationship can be the key ingredient in you becoming more compassionate, more accepting, and a better communicator. Or, in cases where you're dealing with a mate who is clearly reluctant or not invested in the relationship, this difficulty can provide the motivation you need to make a change in your partnership. It is primarily through challenges like these that we grow and make changes in ourselves. If you have a partner who is supremely challenging—congratulations! That means that your future growth is practically guaranteed.

Persuading Your Partner

Structured communication exercises work best with a willing partner. Therefore, when doing them, you must create a context or "container" for the exercise to help get your partner on board. Depending on your partner (and the situation), this can be easy or hard to do. If your partner is in an agreeable mood, it can be as easy as asking: "Could we do a communication exercise for a few minutes?" If your partner is grouchy, resistant, or rolls his or her eyes, your challenge may be much greater. Here are a few suggestions if that happens.

Give your partner a good *reason* for doing the exercise. Explain why you think it's a good idea and what the purpose of the exercise is. You don't need to give a long sermon. You can simply say something like: "We're both getting upset, and I'd like to avoid an argument. Can we try something different?" Or, if you're simply wanting more of a connection, you can say: "I love it when we have deep conversations. It makes me feel closer to you. Can we try something to help with that?"

You can also give your partner a benefit he or she will likely receive by engaging in this kind of practice with you. Try something like this: "I'd like to try a communication exercise with you. It's simple and quick, and I think you'll find I will better understand you and really hear what I've been missing." However you do it, try to convince your partner that it's a good idea to stop what you're both doing and try something different. In order to say "yes" to your request, however, your partner needs additional information—for instance, how *long* this activity will last. After all, it's much easier to agree to a five-minute request than to a fifty-minute request.

On average, women speak about thirteen thousand more words a day than men. Two things happen in a man's brain when a woman says to him: "We need to talk." Initially, he figures he's in some sort of trouble. Of course, that doesn't feel good. Next, he thinks to himself: "This talk is probably going to go on forever." When you set a specific time frame for important communication, it's less daunting. In fact, the idea that a potentially difficult conversation can be over and done with in five minutes may be enticing to your partner and can help you move on to spending time doing the things you love together. So be sure to tell your partner how long an exercise will take. This will make it much easier for him or her to say "yes." Then stick to the time you decided on. I suggest setting a timer. That way, you will both know that you need to focus and that your deliberate communication has a clear endpoint.

If your partner is new to communication methods, explain your chosen exercise in a sentence or two. For instance, if you want to try the Naked Truth exercise in chapter 11, you can say: "I know of an exercise where we disclose what we most like and don't like in sexual play. I think that will help us both enjoy more sexual pleasure."

However you manage it, you need sincere buy-in from your partner before you can begin using these exercises. If you've done your job well up to this point, this should be easy. But sometimes you may need to negotiate. Begin by getting curious and finding out what your partner's initial reaction is. You can ask: "So what do you think? Is there something that would make this more enjoyable or appealing to you?" Listen carefully to the answer. Try to work out something that both partners can agree on.

Here are four simple steps that can help you initiate a communication exercise:

1. State why you want to use an exercise together. Be vulnerable and express what you hope will be achieved by using a communication technique.
2. State how long it will take to do the exercise.
3. State what method you want to use. If your partner is unfamiliar with a technique, explain it in a sentence or two.
4. Ask: "What do you think? Will this work for you or is there some way to make it work for you?"

Although the Simple and Easy Practices given at the end of chapters require no setup, explanation, or rigid structure, because of their spontaneous nature, they are sometimes less effective in achieving a desired result. They do, however, have a couple of advantages over the more formal exercises. First, they can usually be done at almost any time and in just about any situation. This makes them more convenient and easy to use on a daily basis. Second, unlike the structured exercises, the simplified practices do not require your partner's prior commitment. They can be performed spontaneously whenever you feel the time is right. Try both the structured exercises and the simpler practices and see which style best meets your needs.

Overcoming Resistance

Paula often complained that her husband, Rick, avoided intimacy and difficult conversations. Privately, I coached her on how to persuade him into using a communication exercise. I suggested that she pick a time when he was in a good mood and broach the conversation. Paula went home and tried it out. Here's how the conversation went:

Paula: Honey, I'd like to try a little communication exercise with you. It's a way of communicating that's quick, easy, and will help me understand you better. It will also help you to understand me better. It'll only take ten minutes. In it, we take turns telling each other things we've withheld or avoided saying that could be beneficial to know. What do you think? Will this work for you or is there some way to make it work for you?

Rick: I don't want to hear you complaining any more about how I don't communicate. I think I'll pass.

Paula: It sounds as if you're afraid I'm just going to use this as a gripe session. I certainly understand why you wouldn't want to do that. Actually, I want to make it so that we are fully open with each other and don't have any unsaid things that interfere with our connecting more. That's why I'm proposing this ten-minute structured exercise. That way, we can each really hear what the other has to say in a short session, then drop all our complaints and just enjoy each other. If I know you are fully honest with me and I am fully honest with you, we can more easily let go of the past. How's that sound?

Rick: That might be interesting. But I'd rather do this in writing. I don't trust that it's not going to turn into a gripe session.

Paula: We can do it that way. That's a great idea. How about if we each write down three things we want the other person to know about us that we haven't fully communicated before. Then, we'll exchange lists and promise not to give feedback on what we've written. Will that work for you?

Rick: I guess that could work—if it'll cut down on all your nagging.

Paula: I appreciate you being willing to do this. If I get you a pen and paper, are you willing to do it right now?

Rick: Okay.

What I appreciated about Paula's interaction was that she didn't get sidetracked by her husband's snide remarks. I had coached her to listen empathically to what her husband said and work *with* his response rather than criticize his resistance. When Paula's husband initially refused to go along with her idea, she was willing to be flexible and work out something that was mutually agreeable. When couples are able to negotiate like this, they build trust.

Paula later told me that she and Rick were able to glean valuable information from their written feedback. She learned that Rick was feeling lonely and wanted more sexual connection, but he was afraid she'd reject him. Paula disclosed that she felt sad that he was no longer pursuing her sexually, and wanted to be held more. Their newly revealed information freed up a communication log jam that had interfered with their intimacy. The success of this exercise eventually led to his willingness to use other communication methods. (For an exercise that helps reveal withheld information, see chapter 25.)

Once you've done an exercise a couple of times with your mate, your skill at it will develop and you may even find yourself performing it spontaneously and in a matter of seconds. For instance, I often simply say to my wife: "How about a couple of rounds of the appreciation exercise right now?" (You'll find this exercise in chapter 16.) Having done this many times in the past, she already knows the why and what, and knows how long it will take, so we can cut to the chase and immediately begin saying words of love and appreciation. In a matter of moments, we both end up with a good feeling and a deep sense of connection. Once the two of you know how an exercise goes, you may not even need to mention its name. You may just start using it and see if your partner follows along. When I tell my wife in a sincere way that I appreciate her, she normally offers the same feelings back to me out of habit. In this way, we lift each other up with a minimum of imposed structure.

Even though I know how well communication exercises work, I still find that I can resist using them. The parts of me that want to argue, or be right, or play the victim do not want to use these methods. But they really do work extraordinarily well. When I use them, I find that I inevitably have to give up my self-righteousness, blaming, and victimhood. Giving those things up is indeed hard, but being lost in blame and feeling separate from my wife is even harder and more painful. To motivate myself, I sometimes ask myself: "Would I rather do an exercise and be back to love in five minutes, or would I rather be lost in anger and hurt for the next few hours?" Use that question yourself or even pose it to your partner, if it helps.

Another way to overcome resistance to these exercises is to turn them into a ritual. We often perform acts on a regular basis that, if it weren't for the habit of it, would never get done. For example, most people don't love taking their cars in for periodic maintenance and an oil change. We do it because we've decided our cars and our lives go better when we get regular tune-ups. Likewise, you and your partner may decide that the regular "tune-up" provided by a certain exercise makes everything go better in your relationship. If that's the case, simply get together and decide which exercise you'll do and when you'll do it.

A final way to help you and your partner overcome resistance to doing these exercises is to use rewards. By that, I mean reward your partner and yourself immediately after using one of the techniques in this book. You deserve it. After all, the first level of communication is easy. It's like the fast food of communication. It serves a need, but it doesn't truly nourish you. By contrast, communication exercises are more nourishing, although not so easy. It's like working out at the gym. It takes a little bit of effort initially, but you feel great afterward. And, as when you work out at the gym, the more you do it, the more you like it and the easier it gets. The rewards of a physical workout are a healthier body; the benefits of doing these exercises is a healthier relationship—and ultimately more love and less conflict.

A reward can be as simple as a nice meal together. I know a woman who rewards her husband—who normally resists these exercises—with his favorite meal once a week. My wife and I often trade shoulder massages after we do an exercise. Whatever motivates you and your mate to do these exercises on a regular basis is a good idea. After you've done a few of them with your partner, you'll see their amazing benefits. And once that happens, you'll be hooked—and the resistance will disappear.

Flying Solo

Over the years, I've received a lot of emails from people (mostly women) who have said they'd like to practice the methods I suggest—or go to counseling—but their partners are not interested. I generally write back something like: "If you work enough on yourself and your communication, you may be surprised at how much your partner suddenly changes." Technically, this answer is true, but I understand that it's not simple. In fact, it is easier to have good communication and a great relationship when *both* partners are willing to work together. Since that's not always the case, however, I think it's important to discuss what to do when your partner doesn't want to look at this book or use its exercises.

First, I want to acknowledge the frustration you may feel at being in the position where you want to work on your relationship, but your partner does not. That's no fun at all. In fact, if this has been going on for a while, you may feel resentful and even hopeless. Of course, those feelings just add to the sense of separation you may have with your mate, who may pick up on those feelings as well. Yet, there is hope. Rather than trying to change your mate—which you've likely learned is a hopeless endeavor—you can *really* focus on changing yourself. While it may seem unfair that you're "forced" to work on your skills alone, you will indeed become a much better communicator by doing so.

What follows are some tips for how to effectively handle a partner who is seemingly not interested in "working" on the relationship.

Let's Make a Deal

The first approach is simply to find a way to persuade your mate to give these communication exercises (or counseling) a try. How can you do that when what you've tried before has failed? Try something different. In most cases, people try to nag or pressure their partners into reading a book or doing an exercise. That creates a power struggle that usually doesn't end well. Instead, try making a deal with your partner so that both of you get something you want. For example, try suggesting: "If you'd be willing to spend ten minutes doing a communication exercise with me, I'd be happy to give you a ten-minute back massage." Of course, your exact "offering" should be tailor-made to what you are requesting and what your partner finds enticing. If you "make them an offer they can't refuse," you may find your mate is more than happy to make a deal.

When trying to make a deal, I find it helpful to think in terms of trading an equal amount of each other's time. For instance, one woman coaxed her husband into two counseling sessions in exchange for two hours of cooking his favorite meals. It was a win-win for both of them. It is also a good strategy to start small. Your partner may be highly resistant to reading an entire book, but much more open to reading four pages of that book in exchange for something they desire. While you may not like the idea of exchanges or deals, the ability to work out mutually beneficial arrangements is an important relationship skill. With the right attitude, this "deal making" can even become a fun negotiating process. My wife and I often have a lot of laughs as we work out the terms of a deal. She can be a pretty tough negotiator!

Focus on Your Attitudes

A second approach to working with an unwilling partner is to work on yourself. If your partner isn't willing to read this book or do the exercises—or if you don't have a partner right now—focus on your own skills. Of course, you won't be able to do some of the exercises solo, but you can always work on your relationship *attitudes* alone. Back in chapter 3, we discussed the five attitudes that are key for connection: curiosity, generosity, gratitude, vulnerability, and responsibility. I've found that most people have a major lack of skill in one or more of these attitudes. When you markedly improve your ability in one of these attitudes, your partner is clearly impacted. Therein lies your power.

Patty came to my office with the stated goal of "changing her husband." Since her husband wasn't in the office with us, I suggested she work on changing herself. After I asked her some questions, it seemed to me that her weakest attitude was her lack of generosity. She had a lot of complaints about her husband but virtually nothing nice to say about him. I suggested she try a week-long "experiment." I told her to say at least two nice things to her husband every day. Her appreciations had to be truthful, but they could be for things he had done in the past or things she appreciated about him (or his actions) in the present. Patty immediately complained: "But what good will that do?" I explained that we wouldn't know until she tried and that, if she gave it her best shot, it would be interesting to see what happened.

A week later, Patty excitedly returned and said: "I'm married to a completely different man." I didn't know what she meant. She went on to explain: "In the last week, it seems my husband has gone through a total change in attitude." Evidently, her two acts of generosity or appreciation every day for a week had been very impactful. I've seen massive changes like this happen consistently when a single partner decides to really work on his or her "weak leg." Like a couple dancing together, when one partner makes a noticeable change, the other partner is compelled to change as well. Perhaps a week-long "experiment" like this is calling out to you. If so, put Post-it Notes around your house with a coded reminder to jog your memory about the new actions you are committed to taking. Through small actions like these, major changes can occur.

Practice Makes Perfect

When learning any new skill, practice and ongoing motivation are critical. If you don't have a romantic partner, or if your partner is not inclined to do the structured exercises with you, it may be helpful to find someone who will practice with you. This really can be anyone—a friend, a family member, a co-worker. I know one woman who found several "practice partners" when she announced in her church that she was looking for someone to do advanced communication exercises with her. You need not set up a special time or place. The simple habit of responding to people with care, understanding, and empathy will take you a long way toward being a master communicator.

What's the best way to practice without a partner? By focusing on any single method from this book that strikes your fancy—and just doing it. Almost all the exercises given here can be done with friends or family—so not having an available or willing partner need not be an obstacle. Simply find a suitable practice partner, identify a method you want to use, and set up the "container" to do the exercise. You can either have your companion read the exercise with you, or you can explain the basic rules. Or, if you'd rather do things more informally, just use one of the Simple and Easy Practices suggested throughout this book.

Simple and Easy Practice

Use this "fill in the blank" formula to ask your partner to do a communication exercise with you:

- "Honey, I'd like to do a communication exercise with you. It will only take about five minutes. I think it will help us to feel even closer to each other by _____." (Explain in a few words the purpose of the exercise.) "How's that sound to you?"

If you get a "yes," do the exercise immediately. If there is hesitation, ask your partner: "What would make it work for you?"

PART II

Understanding Your Partner

I don't understand your specific kind of crazy, but I do admire your total commitment to it.

ANONYMOUS

The exercises in part 2 revolve around learning more about what makes you and your partner "tick." In my counseling office, I am often surprised at how little couples know about each other—even if they've been married for decades. It's hard for us to truly please our partners if we don't know what they want, what they think, what they like, and what simply annoys them. The exercises here will help you discover things about your partner (and yourself) that can be used to enhance your relationship. The greater your understanding of each other, the greater the chance that you can work together to create a life of joy and harmony.

Knowing what your partner likes, however, is not enough. It's also important to know specifically what your partner finds incredibly annoying. The exercises given here can save you years of needless aggravation and show you how to avoid the pitfalls that threaten most relationships.

CHAPTER 6

Curiosity as a Portal

We know from chapter 3 that curiosity is one of the five key attitudes that leads to more love and less conflict. When you and your partner are stressed, curiosity can prevent you from going down the rabbit hole of blame. It can also be the basis for understanding your mate. After all, if you are truly curious, then you will naturally want to understand how your partner feels and why. In addition, curiosity can help prevent arguments by giving you key information that might otherwise lead to misunderstandings.

When Steve and Erin began to argue over a long-standing jealousy issue, I suggested they try asking each other questions, with the stipulation that neither would respond to the other's answers. Steve began by asking about Sarah's experience of jealousy: "Why do you think I'm attracted to Megan? What does it feel like in your body when you're jealous? What's helpful for me to do when you're feeling really jealous?" Because Steve knew he couldn't respond to Erin's answers, he could really hear her thoughts about this issue—for the first time.

When Steve was done asking his questions, Erin got her chance. Once again, leading with actual curiosity, Sarah was able to find out what was really going on with Steve. She asked: "Have you thought about leaving me for Megan? What's it like for you when I accuse you of flirting with Megan? Has Megan shown you that she's attracted to you?" As Steve answered the questions, trust began to be restored in their relationship. Instead of having a long back-and-forth argument that went nowhere, Erin and Steve were both able to learn valuable new information. Using this new information, they were able to avoid a fight. The conflict was resolved and the love restored.

The following is a simple exercise that can provide you with important information about your partner that can help you avoid conflict and attract more love into your relationship.

I'm Just Curious . . .

After setting up a safe time and space for communication, decide who will go first. Then take five minutes each to ask any questions you want. The only rule is that these questions must be targeted at something you are truly curious about. Each person's job is to answer the questions asked sincerely and honestly. When the first partner's time is up, the other partner gets to ask questions for five minutes. In this way, both partners come to better understand and know each other.

Notice that there is no time allotted for reacting to each other's answers. This exercise is not a conversation. It's a process of discovery that forces you to really listen to what your partner is saying because you don't need to come up with any response. It's also an exercise in restraint, in that, if you're triggered by an answer, you don't have an opportunity to react to it or judge it. It's a great way to circumvent arguments.

Curiosity is a natural ability we are all born with. All we need to do is tune into our natural, childlike tendency to ask questions we want answered. It feels good to be truly curious. We often become so sure that we know everything about our partners that we can get lost in feeling arrogant and uncaring. My wife and I occasionally use this exercise for fun or if we notice that we're not listening to each other very well. It takes us out of the mode of "scoring points" against each other and into the wondrous world of curiosity. The results are often surprising, fascinating, and truly helpful.

Simple and Easy Practice

Curiosity is like a bridge between two people. Recently, I sat next to a ten-year-old girl on an airplane. I decided to start five exchanges with the words: "I'm curious about . . ." For example, I said: "I'm curious about your favorite things to do." Or: "I'm curious about what you're learning in school." After a few minutes of responding to me, she spontaneously started asking *me* questions. In this way, we got to know each other despite our age difference and our different views of the world. Even if you have major differences with your romantic partner, questions coming from true curiosity can help bridge the gap.

CHAPTER 7

Feelings and Desires

Expressing our feelings and desires is a "natural" way of communicating. After all, most four-year-olds are pretty good at stating what they feel and want. It's not complicated. But as we get older and our lives become more complex, we tend to lose this natural ability. We are constrained by our expectations of one another and by the expectations of the society in which we live. Many people feel as if they shouldn't have to tell their partners what they're feeling and what they're wanting. They think their partners should already know. And perhaps they should. But the reality is that they often don't.

When you don't let your partner know directly what you're feeling and wanting, you set your relationship up to fail. After all, your partner is not a mind reader and likely may have a different communication style from yours that makes knowing your innermost feelings and desires that much harder. Of course, just because you state your feelings and desires doesn't mean you always get what you want. But it's certainly a good start.

Good communicators know what they're feeling and wanting and are curious about the feelings and desires of others. The ability to express our own feelings and what we desire is the basis of vulnerability and full self-expression. Knowing the feelings and desires of our partners is the foundation of empathy and our ability to care for them. Unfortunately, this information is rarely expressed directly—partly because it makes us feel vulnerable to do so. A simple communication exercise can help overcome this difficulty, however. I call this exercise: "I'm feeling . . . I'm wanting . . ."

Although this exercise entails simply completing the two sentence prompts "I'm feeling . . ." and "I'm wanting . . . ," to use it to its best effect takes some practice. A good rule of thumb is that your communication should feel vulnerable not self-righteous. A coaching session I had with Cindy and Rob illustrates this point. As you'll see, both Cindy and Rob initially used this technique like a club. But as I coached them to use it correctly, they were able to restore a deep connection. I told them that I wanted them to use this method to express what they were really feeling and wanting and that I'd interrupt them if I sensed they were going off course. Cindy began:

> **Cindy:** I'm feeling that you never listen to me, and I'm wanting you to stop being such an idiot.
>
> **Me:** That's blaming; it's not stating what you really feel and want. Try again, but this time try to be vulnerable in your communication and specific about what you want—not what you don't want.
>
> **Cindy:** I'm feeling . . . hopeless and frustrated. And I'm wanting to feel you care about me.
>
> **Me:** Good. Now Rob, your turn.
>
> **Rob:** I'm feeling fed up with all your complaining, and I'm wanting to be done with all this crap.
>
> **Me:** That is really a criticism. Look deeper and communicate a feeling—for instance, I'm feeling sad, or hurt, or angry, or afraid. Then, say how you would *like* to feel ideally—for

instance, I'm wanting to feel respected, or connected, or loved, or supported, or relaxed.

Rob: I'm feeling . . . hurt and angry, and I'm wanting to feel good.

Me: Can you be more specific? Is feeling "good" wanting to feel loved, or perhaps wanting to feel respected, or maybe something else?

Rob: I think I'm wanting to feel appreciated.

I suggested they try another round.

Cindy: I'm feeling hopeful and curious, and I'm wanting Rob to feel the same way.

Me: If Rob did feel the same way, what would *that* feel like to you? In other words, how do you *want* to feel?

Cindy: I'm wanting to feel more connected with Rob.

Me: And Rob?

Rob: I'm feeling more relaxed and thankful, and I'm wanting to give Cindy a hug.

I explained that Rob's last statement, about wanting to give Cindy a hug, was not a feeling; it was a request. Requests are fine to express in this exercise, as long as they're *positive*. Had Rob said that he wanted Cindy to stop nagging him, that would have been a negative request, and negative requests don't work very well. Our partners take them to be a form of indirect blaming. However, positive requests yield helpful information.

I asked Cindy and Rob to finish the exercise with one more round of what they were feeling and what they were wanting in the frame of a positive request. Cindy began:

Cindy: I'm feeling joyful, and I'm wanting Rob and I to do this practice on a regular basis.

Rob: I'm feeling hopeful, and I'm wanting more hugs like the one we just had.

As you can see, this exercise can communicate really useful information, as well as help to identify things that will make you even happier in your relationship.

At the end of this chapter are two lists: one of thirty common positive feelings and one of thirty common negative feelings. Use them if you have difficulty identifying or naming what you are feeling and wanting as you try using this exercise.

I'm Feeling . . . I'm Wanting . . .

The exercise consists simply of completing two sentence prompts: "I'm feeling . . ." and "I'm wanting . . ." While this may seem easy to do, there are a couple of ways you can do it incorrectly. If you pay attention, however, you'll catch them early. The exercise is not meant to be a way to bludgeon your partner. If you use the exercise to assign blame, you'll go off course. For instance, the following statement is not a true expression of a feeling or a desire: "I'm feeling you're a moron, and I want you to be different." It's an unhelpful complaint. Instead, try saying: "I'm feeling irritated, and I want to feel supported and appreciated by you." The second statement is a vulnerable expression of what you're actually feeling in this moment, as well as what you want to experience.

Here are two lists, one of positive emotions and one of negative emotions, that can help you structure your statements:

Negative Emotions

Afraid

Agitated

Angry

Annoyed

Ashamed

Bitter

Confused

Depressed

Detached

Disappointed

Disgusted

Embarrassed

Exhausted

Fearful

Frustrated

Guilty

Hurt

Impatient

Jealous

Lonely

Miserable

Mournful

Overwhelmed

Resentful

Sad

Suspicious

Upset

Weary

Withdrawn

Worried

Positive Emotions

Affectionate

Amused

Appreciative

Calm

Cheerful

Connected

Content

Curious

Ecstatic

Enthusiastic

Excited

Fulfilled

Grateful

Happy

Hopeful

Invigorated

Loving

Overjoyed

Peaceful

Refreshed

Relaxed

Relieved

Safe

Satisfied

Secure

Stimulated

Tender

Trusting

Warm

Wonderful

Once you've done this exercise and feel as if you understand it, feel free to use its guiding words outside the structured format. For instance, you may say to your partner: "I'm feeling bored watching TV, and I'm wanting to feel more intimate with you. Would you be willing to massage my hand?" In this example, you're combining the "feeling" and "wanting" with a specific request. The phrase "Would you be willing to . . ." can often be a powerful way to turn your dreams into reality. Even if your partner is not willing to do what you request in that moment, he or she may be willing to do something else you like.

I'm not as in touch with my feelings (or desires) as my wife is. Therefore, I've found this practice incredibly helpful. Its open-ended phrases guide me toward revealing critical information that my wife needs to know about me. Sometimes I don't even know what I'm going to say when I begin this exercise. I just start saying "I'm feeling . . ." and wait to see what comes out.

Simple and Easy Practice

Try using the "I'm feeling . . . I'm wanting . . ." technique in small moments during the day with your partner. It can even be something as simple as saying: "I'm feeling stressed, and I'm wanting a hug right now." When you state how you want to feel or what you want from your partner, you give both of you a target to aim for. Once two people concur on an agreeable target, they almost always end up hitting it. Remember, most people want the same things—care, understanding, and empathy. By expressing what you're feeling and wanting with your partner, you'll find that you are able to enjoy these blessings much more often. Look at the lists of positive and negative emotions to help you determine what you currently feel and want, then, at the soonest possible opportunity, let your partner know what you're feeling and wanting— and see what happens.

CHAPTER 8

Pushing Buttons

If I offered you a hundred dollars to make your partner feel upset in under one minute, could you do it? Most people answer an emphatic: "Yes!" To accomplish this, you'd probably just bring up some event, person, or question that invariably irritates your partner. If that didn't work, you could always focus on some perceived fault or shortcoming or some screw-up from the past. There's even a term for this. It's called "pushing buttons." When someone pushes our buttons, it seems we have no choice but to get upset. Over time, partners usually learn what each other's "buttons" are and how to push them.

In this chapter, we'll explore how to use these buttons to bring about positive outcomes. Just as there are automatic ways to get our partners upset, there are also reflexive ways to get them to feel loving. In fact, although most people aren't aware of it, there are ways they can help their partners feel totally loving in under a minute. With the right exploration and technique, you can learn how.

Each person in a relationship can have a very different definition of "true love." Case in point: Many years ago, I had a girlfriend named Bonnie. I was giving her a nice shoulder massage when she suddenly blurted out: "Would you cut that out!" Caught totally off guard, I said: "Cut what out?" "You're always massaging me," she answered. "You're always touching me. Why do you have to be so grabby?" It was true; I frequently massaged her. I told her: "I do that to show that I love you." She quickly responded: "Well, I don't feel very loved. After all, you never tell me you love me." She was right again; I never actually said the words "I love you" to her, although she frequently said those words to me.

Bonnie and I had a long discussion about this exchange and finally realized what had been going on. While I was growing up, whenever I was disciplined or punished, my parents said: "We're doing this because we love you." Therefore, the words "I love you" had a negative connotation for me. I figured that talk was cheap and that the way to show a woman you loved her was to touch her in pleasant ways. That was how I thought real love should be expressed. On the other hand, while Bonnie was growing up, she had an uncle who frequently gave her shoulder massages. One day, this uncle sexually molested her. Therefore, she took my massages as a precursor of impending doom. We both thought we were expressing love to each other, when in fact we were unconsciously pushing each other's buttons!

The way we tend to express love to another person is, in most cases, the way in which we want to receive it. I gave Bonnie massages because that's what makes me feel loved. Even if a gorilla gave me a massage, I'd feel totally loved. Bonnie frequently told me she loved me because that's what she wanted to hear. When people are unaware of their partners' preferred ways of feeling loved, they end up expending a lot of energy that goes unappreciated—or even resented. When you know exactly what helps your partner feel safe and loved, it is infinitely easier to create intimacy on a consistent basis.

In his wonderful book *The Five Love Languages*, Gary Chapman describes the five primary "languages" in which partners give and receive love: words of affirmation, acts of service, receiving gifts, quality time, and physical touch. It's helpful to know your own particular love language, but it's even more useful to understand how your *partner* wants to receive love from you. Here is a simple exercise to reveal this information. You'll need a pen and paper.

How Do I Love Thee?

Remember three specific times you felt completely loved by your partner. Write them down, leaving space in between each observation for another sentence or two. For each time you felt completely loved, go back and write down what it was that helped you to *know* that your partner really loved you in that moment. Be as specific as possible. Here are some examples of how I responded in this exercise:

1. I remember when we were getting married and your eyes were loving and soft and you had an ecstatic look on your face.
   - What made me know that you really loved me was the look of total love emanating from your eyes and the big smile on your face.

2. I remember when you greeted me at the door after a hard business trip and you seemed really glad to see me.
   - What made me realize you loved me was that you had a big smile on your face, your eyes were excited, and you gave me a really juicy hug and a shoulder massage.

3. I remember when we landed in Dubai and started traveling around.
   - What made me realize you loved me was that you had a big smile on your face, and you seemed really

happy. Also, you gave me a lot of hugs and shoulder massages.

As you can see, there are certain repeating themes that indicate to me that my wife really loves me: loving eyes, hugs, shoulder massages, and big smiles. Those are all indications of love to me. What makes my wife feel loved, on the other hand, is actually quite different. By sharing this valuable information with each other, you and your partner will know exactly what "target" to aim for.

At the beginning of a relationship, couples tend do everything to show their love. With so many displays of affection, no wonder you feel loved. However, these efforts are not sustainable over the long term. We begin to take our partners for granted, life gets busy, and children take our attention. On the other hand, if you don't show that you love your partner on a regular basis, your relationship can grow stale. Knowing precisely what helps your partner feel most loved allows you to be smart in how you express your love. This simple little exercise can help both of you to feel a lot more loved with very little additional effort.

Simple and Easy Practice

If you or your partner don't want to do the full written exercise just described, consider using a quick verbal version. At what seems like an appropriate time, simply say to your partner: "I'm curious about something. When was a time that you felt especially loved by me?" When your partner answers, follow up with: "How did you know that I was feeling a lot of love for you at that time?" If it feels right, consider asking other questions about what helps your partner feel loved. For example, ask which "language of love" your partner most appreciates: words of affirmation, acts of service, receiving gifts, quality time, or physical touch.

CHAPTER 9

Avoiding Triggers

When we first fall in love, everything about our partners can cause a warm, glowing feeling. As our relationships mature, however, and we get to know our partners better, we learn things about them that, frankly, drive us crazy—things that can quickly lead to irritation, hurt, and anger. These irritating behaviors and habits are called "triggers." Triggers are very specific behaviors that bother us. If you don't like your partner's weight, that's not a trigger. It's a problem. However, if your partner talks with his or her mouth full and it drives you crazy—that's a trigger.

In my counseling office, I frequently hear partners complain about insignificant things. "He always greets the dog before he says hello to me and it drives me crazy." Or "She's always five minutes late when we need to get somewhere together." It's important to know what some of these triggers are so you can avoid them if possible. But even when you can't avoid them, when you are aware of them, they'll be less likely to create a firestorm.

Here are some examples of triggers clients have identified in sessions with me and my suggestions for how they can avoid them:

- *Trigger:* I don't like it when you speak poorly of my friends or my mother.
  - What I'd prefer you do instead is either say nothing about them at all, or say positive things, or ask me for help with what you're feeling about them.
- *Trigger:* I don't like it when you speak in a whiny, victim-like voice and complain about people in your life.
  - What I'd prefer you do instead is speak in a normal voice about stressful people or ask for help in how to handle them.
- *Trigger:* I don't like it when you're grouchy and yell at me and the dogs in the morning when they jump on the bed.
  - What I'd prefer you do instead is nicely tell me to get the dogs off the bed.
- *Trigger:* I don't like it when you use the words "always" or "never" or "every time" when you're upset with me. For example, the other day you said: "You never take out the garbage without my asking. I always have to ask you—every time."
  - What I'd prefer you do instead is say the words "sometimes" or "frequently" or "rarely."

As you can see in these examples, triggers are specific behaviors that happen at a particular time. The avoidance strategies also point toward a specific action, not a generalized wish. After all, requesting that your partner be nice all the time rather than grumpy is an impossible request, while requesting that he or she ask nicely to get the dogs off the bed has a more reasonable expectation of success. The more precise your feedback and request when dealing with triggers, the more likely it is that your input will be accepted and acted upon.

You may think that your partner already knows what really aggravates you. Not so for most couples. Most of us don't know more than one thing our partners do that triggers a negative response in us—or vice versa. Sometimes the simple sharing of this information can make a world of difference and avoid a lot of conflict. Sometimes, on the other hand, it does not. Habits can be hard to change. But if what bothers you is not a deeply ingrained habit for your partner, there's a good chance he or she will try to avoid doing it. Even if you only avoid conflict half the time, that's still pretty good. Of course, the bad news is that it's not only your partner that needs to change. You need to acknowledge and manage your triggers as well.

I Don't Like It . . . I'd Prefer . . .

Here is a simple five-minute exercise that can help you and your partner avoid a lot of conflict. This exercise is meant to be done on a single occasion and not repeated. Once you and your partner know precisely what bothers each of you the most, you need not ever revisit that information. The technique is especially useful because it offers you and your partner the chance to give each other a *remedy* for each irritation. Because it's often easier to read sensitive feedback as opposed to getting it face to face, this exercise is most effective when written.

Write down four things your mate does that irritate you the most. Have your partner write down the four things *you* do that trigger him or her the most. Begin each trigger with the words: "I don't like it when you . . ." This sentence prompt can be helpful in making your feedback more specific. The words help point you to a precise behavior that happens at a particular time. The idea is that, by knowing what these triggers are, you'll both be better at avoiding them—and/or you'll become less reactive to them.

Be careful not to list judgments or evaluations rather than *behaviors* as triggers. "I don't like it when you're nasty with me" and "I don't like it when you're all uptight" are not specific behaviors. By contrast, "I don't like it when you tell me I'm lazy" and "I don't like it when you won't speak to me all evening" are both precise behaviors. Specific behaviors can be changed; broad evaluations of behaviors cannot. Therefore, make sure your feedback states specific behaviors.

For each of the things you and your partner list as triggers, complete the sentence: "What I'd prefer you do instead is . . ." These words also point you toward something specific. The more precise your feedback and requests, the more likely your input will be taken in. Of course, neither of you may remember or choose to implement these solutions, but at least you'll know what they are. Alternatively, you can ask each other what you are willing to do to avoid triggering negative responses.

Once you and your partner have exchanged your lists of triggers and your written feedback, don't discuss what you've written for at least twenty-four hours. If, after twenty-four hours, either of you have questions, or you want to say something about what you wrote, you can do it then. Hopefully, neither one of you will feel the need, and all you'll have left to do is wait for the positive results.

Simple and Easy Practice

If you are reluctant to give your partner a full list of things that trigger you, consider writing a brief note with a single behavior that bothers you. Simply identify a specific behavior that triggers you and tell your partner what you prefer instead. Be sure to be specific about both. This can be a simple handwritten note placed in an envelope marked "Some useful feedback" or something similar. You don't even need to have any discussion about it. Of course, if your partner brings it up, you can say: "I thought I'd tell you what I prefer so you would know more about me." Then let your partner decide whether or not to change the targeted behavior. The less pressure you bring to bear, the more likely the change will happen.

CHAPTER 10

Know Thyself

Just because we tell our partners what bothers us does not mean they'll refrain from those behaviors. To be fully in control of our destiny, we need to be familiar with what our *own* triggers are—and work to become less reactive to them. Unfortunately, most people are much more familiar with their partner's triggers than their own. This leads them to put all their energy into trying to change their partners rather than changing themselves. This can often lead to a downward spiral that I call the "misery-go-round."

We've all been there. Something we do triggers our partners, and their response then triggers us. Then our response to *their* response triggers us even more—and round and round the whole thing goes. To get off the ride, we can offer care, understanding, and empathy, but it's also useful to explore our own triggers and how they interact with those of our partners. By knowing exactly what those triggers are, we can learn to avoid them, or at least be less reactive to them when they surface.

Everyone has feelings that, when triggered, send them off the deep end. To help you become less reactive to them, it helps to know some key information about the part of you that's triggered.

The more familiar you are with how your trigger "operates," the less likely you'll be to go off half cocked the next time your partner pulls it. For example, what *story* does that part of you tell yourself? What does it typically feel and want? What does it do once it's triggered? And finally, what can you do to recover from it quickly?

To help you understand this process, I'll use a humbling personal example. My wife used to question how much time I spent talking to and visiting my mother. This never failed to send me into a tailspin. On reflection, I realized I had created a story around this that went something like this: "My wife doesn't support me or my family, and I can't live like that." If my wife so much as asked me who I was talking to on the phone, this story played in my mind. I felt hurt and defensive, when what I really wanted was to feel supported by my wife for taking care of my mother. Instead of asking for her support and empathy, however, I lashed out at her for being uncaring. That never helped.

By acknowledging that my mother was a trigger, I became much less reactive whenever the subject came up. When my wife asked me a question about my mother, I simply answered it honestly and moved on. I remained consciously on the lookout for my "mother trigger." And the simple act of anticipating it and knowing how it "operated" was usually enough to disarm it. Try it for yourself. Write down something that triggers you, along with the story you run when that happens. Then explore what you feel, examine what you really want, and consider how you can overcome any reaction when triggered. It can be very powerful.

To help Jessie deal with a trigger that involved his wife, Fran, telling him to clean up after himself, I suggested that he answer what I call the Six Trigger Questions so he could know exactly how this part of himself operated:

Me: What words, tone of voice, or behaviors can you identify that really trigger you?

Jessie: I am triggered when Fran says something like "When are you going to clean up this mess?" in an annoyed, frustrated tone of voice—while I'm in the middle of something that requires my full attention.

Me: When you are triggered in this specific way, what story do you typically tell yourself?

Jessie: I tell myself that my wife is always nagging me and that, whatever I do, it's not enough. I tell myself that I'll always be a victim of her constant complaining.

Me: What feeling do you get after you listen to this story and what are you really wanting?

Jessie: I feel powerless, self-pitying, and annoyed. I want to feel trusted and accepted and have a sense of ease.

Me: What behavior do you typically exhibit once this part of you is triggered?

Jessie: I get whiney; I complain about how she's nagging me. Sometimes I reluctantly pick up a thing or two to satisfy her.

Me: What can you do that will be more effective in getting what you want?

Jessie: I can be proactive and spend a mutually agreed upon amount of time each day cleaning. I can tell Fran to remind me to clean up after myself with Post-it Notes on my desk instead of telling me to do it.

Me: What can you do to be less reactive to this trigger and/or recover from it more quickly?

Jessie: I can anticipate the trigger and watch how it operates. Or I can avoid it by cleaning up before Fran asks me.

I can recover from it more quickly by playing with the dogs once I'm triggered or doing twenty-five jumping jacks to help me let go of the annoyance and sense of powerlessness.

Answering these six questions takes five minutes of intense self-reflection, and self-reflection is really hard work. But by doing this work, you can reduce the amount of time you will be upset in the future. We'd all much rather change our partners than change ourselves. That's understandable. Change is hard. The problem is that when we wait for our partners to change, we are powerless. However, when we work to make ourselves less reactive to what triggers us, we are in control. And there's a bonus. Not only do you suffer less, but your changes will likely be noticed by your partner. Nothing motivates your partner to change more than *you* changing.

Trigger Questions

The next time you find yourself reacting to one of your known triggers, ask yourself these six questions. Be very honest with yourself as you answer them, and take time to reflect on how your answers relate to the specific trigger you are addressing.

1. What words, tone of voice, or behavior are triggering you?
2. When you are triggered in this specific way, what story do you typically tell yourself?
3. What feeling do you get after you listen to this story, and what are you really wanting?
4. What behavior do you typically exhibit once this part of you is triggered?
5. What can you do that will be more effective in getting what you want?

6. What can you do to be less reactive to this trigger and/or recover from it more quickly?

Change is like a virus—it's contagious. But someone has to go first. Your answers to these six questions can be the first step in a process that can significantly alter the patterns in your relationship. Asking yourself these questions can be your step toward getting off the misery-go-round of conflict. Over time, you'll become less reactive to what used to drive you up a wall, and your partner will become less upset at your behavior as well. When you notice your partner becoming less reactive, be sure to praise it. This internal work is hard. People need all the encouragement they can get!

Simple and Easy Practice

If you're not interested in answering all six questions, simply ask yourself: "What's something my partner does that really bothers me?" Then ask: "What can I do when triggered that may work better than what I've done in the past?" It may be as simple as leaving the room and watching a YouTube clip, going for a walk, or taking some deep breaths. Having a couple of ideas ready to go for when the next trigger surfaces can help put you on the road to less triggering and more love.

CHAPTER 11

Honesty Is the Best Policy

We are constantly bombarded by magazines, books, and videos that promote the idea that sexual satisfaction can be had by exploring unusual positions and techniques. Variety, they tell us, is the spice of life. Although trying new things can spice up your love life, I believe the greatest way for couples to improve their sexual satisfaction is by simply telling the truth about their sexual preferences.

The problem for most couples with regard to sex is simply a lack of understanding of their partners' specific needs and desires. By communicating openly about these, two people can vastly improve their sexual experience in a matter of a few minutes. The problem is that most couples find it too embarrassing to talk openly about sex. In this chapter, I describe an exercise that can facilitate the process of communicating honestly about your sexual preferences. I call it the Naked Truth.

In this exercise, partners take turns sharing what they enjoy—and what they don't particularly care for—in their physical relationship. The goal of the exercise is to communicate all the specific things you feel about sex that you might normally be too embarrassed to share. When you do this, you become much more attentive to what truly pleases your lover, and your partner becomes more aware of what is really important to you. To help you better understand this exercise, let's look at how Tom and Linda used it.

Tom: I really enjoy it when you take the initiative in bed by wearing something sexy and "coming on" to me.

Linda: I get very excited when you kiss and hug me a lot after you come home from work. It makes me feel you really love me.

Tom: Sometimes when you kiss me in the morning before brushing your teeth, you have bad breath. I wouldn't mind sometimes being romantic in the morning, but I think you'd need to use one of those breath sprays or mints first.

Linda: Sometimes when you touch me, you are a little rough or use too much pressure. And sometimes you move too quickly. I like it when you take your time and touch me gently and more softly.

Tom: I really enjoy it when you initiate oral sex. It feels fantastic.

Linda: I like it when we spend a while cuddling and you take time stroking my hair before we begin kissing and taking our clothes off.

Tom: I have a hard time when I reach out to you at night and you kind of roll over and don't say anything to me. My feelings get hurt. I guess I'd like for you to say something supportive, even if you don't feel like making love that night.

Linda: I don't know what to do when you want to have sex and I'm not in the mood. I sometimes feel pressured, and that doesn't feel good. I'd like to be able to tell you I'm not in the mood without you taking it so personally.

Tom: I like how you are always willing to listen when I talk about my problems at work and how you get me a beer when I'm tired and want to veg out in front of the TV.

Linda: I really appreciate that you buy me flowers or little things that show me that you care.

Be sure to end this honest exchange on a positive note by sharing something you and your partner appreciate about each other—sexual or otherwise.

The Naked Truth

To perform this exercise, find a comfortable spot to sit with your partner. If possible, play some soft music in the background and hold each other's hands for a couple of minutes in silence. Then agree on who will begin and how long the exercise will continue, either in time or in the number of rounds.

The first partner begins by giving one specific thing he or she enjoys about the other's physical or sexual behavior. When the first partner is done, the other does the same. Then the person who began the exercise points out a precise physical or sexual behavior that he or she doesn't particularly care for. Then the other partner does the same.

Continue to communicate in this manner until both partners have given at least two behaviors they enjoy and two behaviors they don't. End the exercise by both partners describing something they appreciate about the other, sexual or otherwise. Once you have both shared this final appreciative statement, ask each other to clarify anything that you didn't fully understand.

You can also try to solve any issues that arose during the exercise if it feels like the right time to do so. In most cases, men and women have very distinct and different sexual needs and preferences. Therefore, in a spirit of compromise, it's important to try to satisfy your partner's most important desires. By telling the naked truth, you can both move forward toward a more aware, satisfying, and intimate love life.

Simple and Easy Practice

Make sure you initiate any sexual feedback when you are getting along well—and not when you're about to have sex! You can say something like: "Is it okay if I tell you something I really like about our sexual connection and something that would make it stronger?" If your partner responds well to this inquiry, you can proceed. I suggest you start with what you'd like to improve first, so that you can end on a good note. You can begin by filling in the sentence: "I don't particularly like it (or it troubles me) when you . . ." Once that feedback is given, immediately describe the positive behavior you *do* like. Then, if appropriate, end by saying: "Do you have any sexual feedback you'd like to share with me?"

CHAPTER 12

Your Perfect Partner

I have two dolls that I often use in my workshops. Their names are Mr. and Mrs. Wonderful. When you squeeze them, they each say things the opposite sex would love to hear—but never gets to hear. For example, Mr. Wonderful says: "Thinking of you is the best part of my whole day!" Mrs. Wonderful says: "Don't worry honey; I forgot it was our anniversary, too." Well, I've got good news and bad news. The bad news is that Mr. and Mrs. Wonderful don't exist in real life. The good news is that I can give you an exercise that will allow you and your partner to enjoy the next best thing. In this exercise, you tell your partner exactly what you'd *like* them to say (and/or do) in a specific situation. Relationship coach Kamala-devi (*Kamaladevi.com*) shared this technique with me, and I've found it to be both effective and fun.

To understand how the exercise works, let's look at how two of my clients used it. Monica and Jim came to me, each complaining about how the other handled their kids. Monica had a lot of resentment toward Jim because he sometimes yelled at them, and she didn't think that was a good idea. Jim, on the other hand, had a lot of resentment toward Monica because he felt she was a terrible disciplinarian and that the kids were out of control. Each had spent years feeling that their concerns went unheard, and the blame and resentment persisted. I suggested they try this exercise. I told them both to write down all the things they secretly *wanted* each other to say about how they were handling their kids. Here is what each one wrote:

> ***What Monica wants Jim to say***: Honey, I see that your job is so very hard. I know how much you love the kids, and how much it bothers you when they act poorly. I understand that it pains you when you have to punish them even a little bit and that, when I yell at them, it causes you a lot of pain. I'm so sorry for all the pain I've caused you and the kids. Perhaps you're right that it's a mistake to yell at them. It clearly hasn't worked out well. We really need to get some professional help to make sure our kids don't end up even more out of control. We really need to work together so that the kids we both love can grow up to be mature, caring adults. Come here and give me a hug. I'm committed to doing whatever it takes to make sure the kids are okay. I love you and the kids very much.

> ***What Jim wants Monica to say***: Sweetie, I recognize that the kids have been out of control lately. I'm sorry. I feel largely responsible because, with the amount I'm working now, I don't have the time and energy to be there for them as much as I used to. I know I've blamed you for yelling at the kids, and while I still don't like it, I doubt that's been the problem. I think neither one of us really knows what to do, and that maybe we need to seek out some professional help or a book to get some new ideas. But I understand that you really love the kids and that you're committed to doing whatever is needed to get them back on track. Together, I know we can do that.

Notice that Monica and Jim's words shared several important themes. They both wanted acknowledgment for the hardship they were going through. In addition, each wanted the other to take some responsibility for the difficulties they'd been having. Finally, they both agreed that getting outside help could be a good thing.

Just reading the words they'd written for their "perfect partners" seemed to make Monica and Jim feel better. I pointed out that they each wanted the same things—empathy for the hardships they'd been through and a desire that the other take some responsibility. That made them feel even more united. I also pointed out that their perfect partners' statements contained an indirect description of what they really *wanted* from each other—care, understanding, and empathy.

Mr. and Mrs. Wonderful

This exercise involves you and your partner writing down all the things you secretly *want* each other to say about a given situation. This seems simple, but there are some things to beware of when doing it.

First, reading your partner's statement can sometimes be very triggering. After all, you're reading about a sensitive issue, so that alone can be difficult. In addition, your mate may have "you" (the "perfect partner you") apologize or take responsibility in ways you find upsetting. Therefore, it's critical to remember why and how this information can help your relationship. Your partner is telling you what he or she most needs from you to get to a place of forgiveness and love. When this exercise is done in the right spirit, however, its healing and informational benefits far outweigh any risks involved. To minimize the risks involved, agree beforehand that you won't say anything about your partner's written thoughts for at least twenty-four hours.

If you feel called to do this exercise, simply imagine what your perfect partner would say and do in relation to a sensitive issue you have. Write out your response in detail, even including any way you'd like to be touched or held. Many of my clients have said that just reading what they wrote to themselves made them feel better—even before they exchanged pages with their partners.

For me, the most impactful aspect of this exercise is that couples learn in detail what their partners are really wanting from them. This information is incredibly valuable whenever sensitive issues arise. So the next time a volatile issue comes up, use this exercise to get a clearer idea of how you can be a perfect partner for your mate.

Simple and Easy Practice

Whenever you feel hurt or upset by something your partner did, ask yourself: "What would I have liked my perfect partner to say or do in this situation?" Then ask yourself: "If my partner said or did that, what desire would that have fulfilled in me?" (Look at the Universal Desires listed at the end of chapter 2 for help with this). For example, if you want your perfect partner to apologize sincerely to you, perhaps that fulfills your desire for more trust or respect. Once you know what you truly desire from your partner, it will be easier to ask for what you want directly. You can say something like: "What I really desire is to feel more trust with you and to feel more respected."

CHAPTER 13

Shared Pleasures

In any long-term relationship, couples often get into ruts. These "grooves" can zap the passion and excitement out of your connection. It has been said that the only difference between a groove and a grave is a couple of feet! What can you do to avoid this rut? You can add variety to your time together. Rather than falling into the same old routine of dinner and a movie, you can continually seek out new activities that are both fun and fulfilling. In order to do this, however, it's important to have a list of activities from which to choose. Otherwise, you'll be tempted just to go with what's easy rather than exploring what's possible.

The exercise in this chapter consists simply of making lists of things you want to do with your partner. Here are the lists a couple named John and Brenda made of things they wanted to do together.

John's List

Go golfing (miniature or regular)

Travel to New York City

Go to a football or basketball game

See a rock concert

Take dogs to a dog park

Go to a workshop on Tantra

Camp in a national park

Smoke marijuana

Rent a speedboat

Go to a Burning Man festival

Brenda's List

See the ballet

See a movie

Visit Yosemite

Buy a new couch

See a concert together

See a famous comedian

Go to Hawaii

Rent a jet ski

Remodel the kitchen

Go bowling

Although on the surface it looks as if John and Brenda's lists don't have much in common, this actually isn't true. Although the only "direct" matches were John's desire to go to a national park and a rock concert and Brenda's desire to go to Yosemite and a concert, when they looked over their lists, they saw more potential matches. They both liked the idea of doing a sport together. They both liked the idea of traveling. And they both wanted to rent some kind of water craft (speedboat vs. jet ski). In addition, although John included items that were not on Brenda's list, some of his items were exciting to her. John was quite surprised that she was willing to smoke marijuana with him or visit New York City.

Adventure, fun, and play are important ingredients of a successful partnership. Couples that play together tend to stay together. Creating lists of things you want to do is easy and quick and offers a doorway to more passion, fun, and adventure. Furthermore, planning something fun together will give the two of you something to look forward to.

In addition to doing activities that you enjoy together, look for ways to keep laughter and play in your relationship. The more laughter you can bring into your relationship, the stronger it will likely become. Fortunately, nowadays you don't need to be Jerry Seinfeld to make use of the magical properties of humor. You can simply watch YouTube clips of comedians like Seinfeld, or Kevin Hart, or Ellen Degeneres. I know many couples that start off their date night by showing each other humorous YouTube clips or by sharing funny stories from their week.

The key is being willing to give yourself *permission* to be funny and to have fun. No grand plan required. Sometimes your attempts will fall flat, but it's worth the risk. While most of the methods in this book have a certain seriousness about them, intimacy and love also grow through humor and play. In today's overly serious and stressful world, we need all the humor and play we can get. If telling funny stories from your week or watching comedic YouTube clips works for both of you, consider making it a weekly ritual.

Play Together; Stay Together

The following technique will help you to explore new and potentially fun pursuits you can do with your partner. In this written exercise, you and your mate come up with ten things you want to do with each other. These can be things you've done in the past or new things you want to try. Once you each have a list of ten items, exchange lists and see where there's commonality.

You get a lot of bang for your buck from this simple five-minute exercise. Once you have some items that you each agree will be fun to pursue, you have a common mission. The next step is to plan your outing together—which should bond you even more. You may even be able to negotiate to do one of your partner's preferred activities if he or she does one of yours. In the case of John and Brenda, Brenda was willing to go golfing if John was willing to go bowling with her.

Once you have an idea of something you'd both like to do together, schedule it. Actually put it on your calendar, so you are committed to doing it. The activity can be something simple, like a couples' massage or perhaps arranging a babysitter so you can go for a hike together. The important thing is that you schedule the activity so you can kick-start the fun.

Simple and Easy Practice

If getting your partner to sit down to write out a list is like pulling teeth, here's another option. During a time of pleasant connection with your mate, say something like: "I'm curious as to what you'd say are your five favorite things to do at this point in your life." If one of the things mentioned is something you'd like to do as well, let your partner know it. Then share five things you want to do and see if your partner is interested in doing any of those activities with you. If you agree on something, don't forget to commit to it by putting it on your calendar.

CHAPTER 14

The Real You

A couple of years ago, I went to a workshop at which we were told to get into groups of four. Then we were instructed to take turns completing this sentence: "If you really knew me . . ." No other instructions were given. At first, participants offered general statements like: "If you really knew me, you'd know I'm really shy." But a few minutes later, participants were offering statements like: "If you really knew me, you'd know I tried to commit suicide last month." All kinds of intense truths started coming out. I was amazed. Within five minutes of meeting, these total strangers became incredibly open and vulnerable with each other.

I've used this method in my communication seminars. It never fails to lead to a quick dive into vulnerability, intimacy, and depth. When couples use this practice, partners often learn more about each other in five minutes than they normally learn about each other in a year. A variety of information can come out during this exercise, from the vulnerable and deep to the superficial and stupid. Here are examples of the range of answers I've seen revealed:

- If you really knew me, you'd know I love writing.
- If you really knew me, you'd know I love being a teacher because it makes me feel important.
- If you really knew me, you'd know I'm not as good a communicator as I feel I should be.
- If you really knew me, you'd know I feel self-conscious about the size of my nose.
- If you really knew me, you'd know I think I'm very funny.
- If you really knew me, you'd know I'm afraid of coming off as arrogant.

There's something about the simplicity of this exercise and the rhythm of completing the same sentence over and over that has a disarming effect. If you have the courage to try it with your partner or even a friend, you'll see what I mean.

If You Really Knew Me . . .

Other than being honest in your answers and deciding how long you'll continue the exercise, there's really not much more to say about it. You can answer at whatever level of self-disclosure you want. Even two minutes of doing this exercise can be very powerful.

First decide how many rounds you will complete or how much time you will spend on this exercise, then simply go back and forth with your partner completing the sentence: "If you really knew me . . ." Try not to think about your answers too much. Just blurt out the first things that come to mind. Be sure not to comment on your partner's answers.

It's a good idea to decide before starting if any discussion or comments about what is revealed will be allowed after the exercise is over. I've seen couples who prefer a time for comments, and I've seen couples who don't. Choose what feels right for both of you.

After a number of rounds with your partner, I think you'll both find this exercise to be a deeply rewarding experience. Not only does it get things "off your chest," it also breaks down the invisible walls that often keep us from deeper intimacy.

Simple and Easy Practice

Rather than setting up a specific number of rounds—or even explaining the method to your partner—just jump right in. Finish the sentence: "Something you may not know about me is . . ." Once you have said something that is a bit vulnerable, ask your partner: "What is something I may not know about you?" Or perhaps just look for little opportunities to reveal things about yourself in the moment. For example, you may complete the sentence: "Right now, I'm thinking . . ." Or perhaps: "Right now, I wish I felt . . ." These simple sentence prompts can be launching pads for more intimacy, vulnerability, and a deepening of connection. From them, you can often achieve a deep sense of intimacy.

PART III

Increasing Love in Your Relationship

All you need is love. But a little chocolate now and then doesn't hurt.

CHARLES SCHULTZ

The exercises in part 3 are designed to bring more warmth and depth to your communications by creating more trust, safety, and intimacy. When you have an abundance of trust and safety with your mate, almost anything you say will go over well. The opposite is also true, however. When there's a lack of trust and safety in your relationship, anything you say may be met with suspicion. So it's important to make sure you always have a reservoir of trust and safety to draw upon.

Whenever two people's lives are intertwined, they share an "emotional bank account." When there's an abundance of trust, safety, and care between them, their joint "account balance" is high. When there is disagreement, hurt, or poor communication between them, this emotional bank balance can dwindle. In the case of divorce or the ending of a friendship, it's as if the two people are declaring bankruptcy. To avoid bankruptcy, you must always be making deposits into your shared account in preparation for the occasional problems (withdrawals) that inevitably arise in any long-term relationship. The exercises in part 3 will help you to make these "deposits."

CHAPTER 15

Say What You See

Have you ever met someone who seems to really understand you—to really "get" you? It's a great experience when someone gives you the gift of their full and complete presence. Whenever I meet someone who displays this ability, I try to decipher exactly how they create such magic. I have two friends, Scott and Emily, who are extremely good at making you feel that you're the most important person on Earth when you talk to them. While they do many subtle things to create this impression, the most important thing they do is to speak up about the things they notice.

I built on this simple technique to create an exercise I call "I notice . . . I imagine . . . ," in which couples begin by making observations based in the present moment. The observations you make here should be statements of fact not impressions. For instance, to say "I notice that you're upset" is really an interpretation, whereas saying "I notice that you're yelling at the dog" is more clearly based on observable fact. As you say what you notice about your partner in the present moment, you create a potential moment of intimacy and connection. Then, by saying what you imagine about your partner, you create a "shared reality" with them. This is level 3 communication—the most intimate kind.

In watching couples in my office use this technique, I have been struck by the fact that what they "notice" may be accurate, but that frequently what they "imagine" about each other is clearly wrong. We typically *assume* that we know what's going on in our partners' heads. After using this exercise a few times, however, you soon learn that your odds of being right are probably only about 50/50. But you also learn that, even when you guess wrong about your partner's experience, your efforts are still appreciated. After all, the effort to imagine someone's experience indicates that you care; and, although you may have guessed wrong, at least now your partner has an opportunity to set you straight.

To get a better grasp of how this technique works, consider how Mike and Jenny used it.

> **Mike:** I notice you're tearing up, and I imagine you're feeling sad because we haven't had time to connect lately.
>
> **Jenny:** Actually, I'm feeling a lot of love for you for being willing to sit down and do this practice with me.
>
> **Mike:** That's nice to hear.
>
> **Jenny:** I notice that your face is relaxing and you just took a deep breath, and I imagine you're feeling relieved because you've been feeling guilty for having to work a lot lately. Is that what's going on for you?
>
> **Mike:** That's correct.
>
> (Round two)
>
> **Jenny:** I notice you're avoiding eye contact with me, and I imagine you are feeling a bit uncomfortable doing this exercise.

Mike: That's correct. I notice that your eyes are shining, and I imagine that you're feeling appreciative of me for being willing to connect with you in this way.

Jenny: That's right.

From this brief exchange, Mike and Jenny went from feeling separate to feeling very connected, ending the exercise with a hug. Once their emotional connection was reestablished, their future communications that day were sure to go more smoothly. In addition, because they became familiar with this method, they will now likely remember to use "I notice . . . I imagine . . ." statements at appropriate times in the future. Whenever "I notice" and "I imagine" statements are used, a shared reality is immediately created—and this is a necessary prerequisite for true intimacy. Without it, two people are often lost in their own worlds—not even realizing that they're not really connected.

I Notice . . . I Imagine . . .

Using this exercise in a structured manner with your partner involves three simple steps. First, decide how many rounds you'll do and who will go first. Then say what you notice and imagine to your partner. Finally, have your partner respond to what you say with either the words "That's correct" or with a report of what he or she is really experiencing or feeling. For example, you may say: "I notice your forehead is furrowed . . ." Or: "I notice you seem irritated . . ." Or you can make an observation about yourself: "I notice I'm tired and distracted . . ." Or: "I notice I'm feeling a lot of love for you . . ." Simply by saying the words "I notice . . . ," you ground your communication in the present moment and show that you're willing to be vulnerable.

Next, state what you imagine to be true about what you just noticed. What you noticed and your thoughts on it may be something external to both of you, for instance: "I notice it's after midnight, and I imagine you want to go to sleep." Or you may make an observation about yourself: "I notice I'm not giving you my full attention, and I imagine that you're feeling irritated by that." Or you may make an observation about your partner: "I notice you seem upset, and I imagine it's because I got home late." You can get bonus points for asking your partner, "Am I correct?" once you've said what you imagine to be true for them. These statements all give your partner an invitation to respond to the accuracy or falseness of your communication. By saying what you imagine, you establish the "shared reality" without which true intimacy cannot flouish.

Simple and Easy Practice

You can use a quick, unstructured version of this exercise to keep yourself out of trouble. Simply say something like: "I notice you didn't give me a morning hug, and I imagine you're upset with me." If your partner doesn't respond, you can always ask: "So, was I correct?" Even though what you imagine may be wrong, it's great to share your thoughts. When you forget to do that, you can spend the rest of the day imagining your partner is upset with you, when in reality the problem relates to something at their work. And if your partner really *is* upset with you, at least you will have given him or her a chance to talk about what's going on—rather than letting it simmer and create distance.

CHAPTER 16

Say What You Like

In chapter 3, we discussed studies that showed that the single best predictor of how happy a couple reports themselves to be is the number of appreciative statements they make to each other. Other things that you may think of as good predictors—money, youth, common interests, or health status—seem to make much less difference. That's the good news. You can't always acquire more money, improve your health, or change other factors in your relationship, but you can always express more appreciation to your partner.

The bad news is that, as two people live with each other, they often become painfully aware of all the little things each does that annoy the other. The human mind is like Velcro for negativity, but like Teflon for positivity. The things we dislike about our partners tend to stick to us and be very noticeable, while the things that originally attracted us to them can slip away. The exercise in this chapter can help to rebalance the scales.

Not all demonstrations of appreciation have equal weight or value, however. For instance, if I tell my wife that I appreciate that she is healthy, that may have minimal impact. After all, my wife already knows she has good health, so my comments don't mean much to her. On the other hand, if I say something more specific and less obvious, my comments are likely to have more effect. For instance: "I love the way you take great care of your body. I feel proud every time I look at you—your gorgeous hair, your shiny eyes, your great figure. I'm so lucky to be married to a woman who is so beautiful inside and out." Specific and heartfelt comments like this can be much more impactful.

Sometimes when I discuss appreciation at my workshops, people worry that it will come off as insincere flattery—and that's a valid concern. A good rule of thumb is that you should never express any appreciation that you don't truly think and feel. However, it has been my experience that voicing insincere flattery is not a common problem. A bigger problem is that partners simply don't express much appreciation at all. When we appreciate our mates, it can make us feel vulnerable. In addition, accumulated resentments can get in the way of acknowledging that for which you are truly grateful. Couples often play a kind of waiting game in which they secretly wait for their partners to be the first to say what they appreciate. The result of this unfortunate game is that they rarely express their warm feelings for each other, and both lose out.

The exercise below gives you a simple way to make expressing what you love about your partner an ongoing habit. There are many benefits that can result from its use. First, what you focus on grows. As we look for and express things we appreciate about our partners, we find even more things we like about them. Second, as our partners express what they appreciate about us, we learn what it is about us that *they* most enjoy. That's important information! Then we know to do more of those things.

Finally, for couples having a hard time, nothing is as effective as telling each other something nice. When two people are hurting inside and/or arguing a lot, all communication can become difficult. We've all been there. What people really need at such times are appreciation and love. This exercise offers both partners an emergency dose of what they need. Once care and appreciation are restored, all other attempts at communication are much more likely to go well.

The exercise consists of partners simply taking turns completing the sentence prompt "I appreciate . . ." Here's an example of Daniel and Vanessa using the exercise.

> **Vanessa:** I appreciate that you took out the garbage last night. It makes me feel proud and taken care of when you do chores like that without me having to remind you.
>
> **Daniel:** Thank you. I appreciate how you greeted me at the door last night with a kiss and a hug. You seemed happy to see me, and that always makes me feel good.
>
> **Vanessa:** Thank you. I appreciate how you're always on time. It makes me trust you and makes it so I don't have to worry about when you'll show up. That means a lot to me.
>
> **Daniel:** Thank you. I appreciate that you're always very accepting of my friends when they come over to watch football. I know sometimes they can be loud and messy when they come over, but you take it in stride and have a really good attitude about it. That means a lot to me, and I feel proud when my friends comment that I have "a cool wife."

David and Vanessa's exchange illustrates that appreciation can be expressed for specific or recent behavior, as well as for character traits, attitudes, or abilities. Appreciating a variety of things about your partner has more power and impact than simply one type of positive feedback. Acknowledging the deeper traits of your partner that you admire—generosity, wisdom, or compassion—has more impact that just appreciating simple behaviors.

I Appreciate . . . Thank You

I suggest couples do this exercise a minimum of once a week. Knowing that you'll be doing it regularly helps train your brain to look for things you really do—or could—appreciate about your partner. You don't need to like everything about your mate before you express appreciation for a specific trait, action, or characteristic that you admire. However, as you express what you appreciate, you'll likely find that what you admire becomes even more prevalent and noticeable.

Here are a few guidelines for the exercise:

1. Eliminate any distractions you can—turn off the TV, mute your phone.

2. Sit facing your partner. If it feels right, hold hands and/ or look into each other's eyes.

3. Decide on the number of rounds you'll go through. Either partner may begin.

4. One partner begins by saying something he or she appreciates about the other, either a recent behavior or a general characteristic.

5. The second partner says "Thank you" and then shares what he or she appreciates about the other—again, either a recent behavior or a general trait.

6. Whenever possible, be specific about what you like, and even include how what you appreciate about your partner makes you feel.

7. Always end with a hug.

This exercise can be a great way to bond with your partner quickly and can also help a couple get through a difficult time. In fact, it may be the most important technique a couple can use when going through a hard time, because it tends to soften and open the heart. And from an open heart, care, understanding, and empathy are restored. Sometimes the intimacy created in this exercise can lead organically to more conversations or more physical connection. Now that's a benefit anyone can appreciate.

Simple and Easy Practice

Don't just leave it to "exercise time" to say what you like about your partner. Let your words of appreciation flow spontaneously whenever you feel them or remember to say them. You can also use texts, love notes, emails, or voicemails of appreciation. The more frequently you express your appreciation, the more loved your partner will feel. A wonderful couple I know, Sonika and Christian, suggest in their workshops (*loveworksforyou.com*) saying one appreciation before sleep every evening. Even if what you appreciate is something small, communicate it. Get into the habit of saying sentences that start with the words "I appreciate . . ." or "I love it when you . . ." As you communicate these sentiments, watch a virtual stream of love begin to flow between the two of you.

CHAPTER 17

Ask for Answers

As we discussed in chapter 6, I strongly believe in the power of asking good questions. In fact, I wrote a book that consisted mostly of thought-provoking questions called *Life's Big Questions*. We all like to talk about ourselves and, if you ask your partner (or really anyone) a good question, it opens the door to deeper connection. Over the years, I've experimented with dozens of questions to determine their effect on people. Eventually, I came up with two lists of fifteen questions that have been shown to have a highly positive effect on the couples who answer them.

The first set of questions I call Deeper Intimacy Questions. These can help couples feel more vulnerable and connected to each other and are best used when you want to create a more heartfelt connection with your partner. The second set of questions I call Empathic Understanding Questions. These are aimed at helping two people have a greater understanding of each other. Both sets create a feeling of deep connection and can also be used with friends or family members. Moreover, any of these questions can be used to spark a profound conversation. You can spontaneously ask your lover, friend, or family member *any* of these questions at any time.

The questions in these lists form the basis of this chapter's exercise, which is designed to help you get to know someone on a fairly intimate level. The questions can be answered at whatever degree of self-disclosure you wish. If you give this exercise enough time and sincerity, I'm confident you'll find it to be a very satisfying experience.

What . . . ?

This is an exercise that can evoke a powerful response, so be sure to create a sacred space for your exploration. These questions deserve plenty of time and your full focus. Find a quiet place, turn off your phone, and perhaps even light a candle to create a safe space. Set aside up to an hour to answer all fifteen questions, although you may only need a half hour or forty-five minutes.

Take as long as you like to answer each question. Once you're done answering a question, pose the same question to your partner. When you're the one asking a question, feel free to ask related questions that may further clarify or expand upon your partner's initial response. If a brief conversation naturally unfolds from your partner's response, that's perfectly all right as well.

Deeper Intimacy Questions
1. What makes you feel most affectionate?
2. What was your first impression of me?
3. What do you like best about me?
4. What's one of your darkest secrets?
5. What do you want me to know about you?
6. What helps you to feel really loved?
7. What are you avoiding saying to me?
8. What do you notice about yourself when you're with me?

9. What was the last thing that made you cry? Why?

10. What frightens you about intimacy?

11. What's the most important thing you've learned about sex?

12. What do you think I think about you?

13. What makes you feel most connected to me?

14. What do you wish you could share with someone you love?

15. What do you feel right now?

Empathic Understanding Questions

1. What do you do to try to impress people or get them to like you?

2. What would your inner child say if he/she could speak?

3. What is something you've been learning about yourself?

4. What is your "superpower"?

5. What is your "kryptonite"?

6. What does a perfect day look like to you?

7. What do you feel the most gratitude for?

8. What is one thing you're ashamed of?

9. What is one thing you really "get" or understand about me?

10. What do you really like about yourself?

11. What was the most challenging time in your life? Why?

12. What is something you feel is missing in your life?

13. What event would you say shaped your life the most?

14. What is something that really scares you?

15. What makes you the happiest?

When doing this structured exercise, use each list of questions separately, as each aims at a different aspect of your relationship. The intimacy questions target connection; the empathy questions target understanding. The exercise will be more powerful if you stay focused on one goal.

Simple and Easy Practice

It can be challenging to set aside up to an hour to address all fifteen questions from either list. The good news is that you don't have to. Every question on each of the lists is a powerful way to create a deeper connection with your partner. Simply choose any question beforehand and—perhaps over dinner or while driving in the car together—say something like: "There's a question I have for you that I'm curious about." Then ask a single question from either of the lists. After your partner answers, you can offer up your own reply if it feels right to do so. Once a deeper conversation has been started, feel free to keep it going in whatever way feels appropriate.

CHAPTER 18

Perform Periodic Maintenance

When couples ask me which technique I recommend for regular "relationship maintenance," I usually suggest a technique I call the "Relationship Tune-up." Used once a week, this exercise can provide each partner in a relationship with a lot of useful information. In just a few minutes, it can clear out any "cobwebs" and help couples start out each new week with a clear, informed, caring attitude.

The exercise consists of completing five sentence prompts:

1. The best thing that happened to me this week was . . .
2. Something I've been feeling lately is . . .
3. Something I've been wanting lately is . . .
4. The time I felt most connected to you recently was . . .
5. Something I appreciate about you (or have appreciated about you recently) is . . .

Instead of giving you an example of a couple using this technique, I will briefly explain why each of these five sentence prompts can provide powerful information to partners seeking to maintain a healthy relationship.

The first sentence prompt encourages couples to look back and celebrate life's good moments together. In fact, research shows that, when couples acknowledge and celebrate each other's victories, it helps to create a lasting bond. Couples who fail to recognize life's good moments together end up spending more time arguing. By completing this sentence, you automatically create a moment of positive connection with your partner.

The second and third prompts help to uncover what each partner is feeling and wanting. Knowing how you feel and what you want are possibly the two most important pieces of information you can reveal to your partner and to yourself. Like a good map, this information discloses exactly where you are and where you want to go. We often get so lost in our heads that we forget the power and simplicity of knowing the direction we want to take. Once you've defined where you are and where you want to be, it's much easier to hit your intended target.

The fourth prompt has two purposes. First, it helps you remember a special moment you recently had with your partner. We tend to remember the bad moments more than the good ones, so this prompt helps you remember (and perhaps reexperience) a good moment. That by itself can be strong medicine. Moreover, by completing this sentence, you indirectly inform your mate of the *type* of moments you really appreciate and enjoy together. That information will help your partner know what you truly value and make it more likely he or she will create more moments like it in the future.

The fifth prompt focuses on appreciation and provides a great way to end the exercise on a positive note. As I've mentioned before, one of the best predictors of a happy relationship is the amount of appreciation partners express to each other. When partners share what they appreciate about each other, it makes both of them feel good. It also tends to be the most powerful way to actually *change* behavior in a positive direction. I tell my clients that praising their partners when they do something "right" is a hundred times more effective in getting them to change than nagging them to be different.

Relationship Tune-up

First, read and become familiar with the five sentence prompts given above. Alternatively, you can write them on a small card and use that as a reference during the exercise. Before you begin, make sure you are in a comfortable private place where you can relax and focus. After one partner completes the first sentence prompt, the other one completes the same sentence. Alternate completing the prompts until both partners have completed all five sentences. If you prefer, and agree to it beforehand, you can ask each other questions during the exercise to get more information. I've seen this technique take as little as five minutes or as long as half an hour. It all depends on how much time and curiosity you and your partner have.

This exercise can also be used effectively with close friends. In any relationship, it allows you to catch up quickly and create a good foundation for further connection. I've found that this exercise is very effective for couples who have little time but share a strong desire to connect deeply and intimately. If you try it and it works well for you and your mate, consider coming up with a weekly time during which you'll use it. I know of many couples that use it as part of their date night, while others use it on Sunday night as a way to complete their week. Whenever you use it, I think you'll find it to be a simple but powerful tonic that encourages togetherness.

Simple and Easy Practice

If you don't have time for the entire five-sentence series, try engaging your mate with just one of the prompts. For example, while at dinner, ask: "What has been the best thing that happened to you this week?" When your partner is done speaking, share your own response to that question. By doing this, you can easily deepen your communication from level 1 (informational) to level 2 (emotional/personal).

CHAPTER 19

Spoon 'Til You're Tuned

When you're really upset with your partner, using any of the methods in this book can be difficult. In fact, the more intense your emotions, the less verbally skilled you are likely to become. That's why I've offered a few methods that don't require any verbal dexterity. Sometimes what's needed is to create a connection that doesn't depend on words. The Spoon Tune is such a method. It bypasses the verbal brain and instead makes use of a more primitive part of your brain. By helping you go beyond your normal fight, flee, or freeze reaction to stress, this practice makes you feel connected to your partner—even when you *want* to stay upset.

We live in a culture that values words. Yet words are only one way of solving problems and feeling connected to our partners. The body has its own wisdom. As when a couple makes love, the body has ways of enjoying connection that go way beyond words. When you use the Spoon Tune technique, you'll see that overcoming upsets and connecting is as easy as a hug and a breath away.

The method is simple. You make a deal with your partner that, whenever either one of you makes a request to "breathe together," you'll stop what you're doing and perform this exercise. The exercise involves partners either hugging or spooning (one person's front to the other's back). Either way is fine. Once the couple is hugging or spooning, the man matches his breathing pattern to the woman's. That's it.

The result of this seemingly innocuous technique is rather amazing, however. No matter how upset you are at your partner when beginning this exercise, your upset will quickly fade. Your body will feel comforted by the hug, and your mind will become occupied with the coordinated breathing. The fact that you're breathing together will also help put the two of you on the same energetic "wavelength." Almost as if by magic, you'll soon be able to let go of your upset and feel connected to your partner once again.

The Spoon Tune is useful for more than just calming upsets. It's also a great way to let go of stress when you first come home from a day at work or to connect with your partner at the beginning of a date. It works whether you think it will or not. It works when you're angry; it works when you're frustrated; it works when you feel good; it works even when you don't want it to work. Try it, and you'll see what I mean.

Spoon Tune

The hardest part of this exercise is getting people to try it for the first time. When you're upset, you probably don't want to hug your partner. Do it anyway. Make an iron-clad agreement that, if either of you says "Let's breathe together," you'll do it for at least three minutes. Agree beforehand on whether you will hug or spoon—either way is fine and both work well, although some couples prefer one over the other. Spooning is a bit less intimate, and therefore easier for some to do at first. Alternatively, if you're near a bed, you may choose to do the exercise lying down. Whatever helps you to feel comfortable is fine.

Since the two of you will be holding each other, it should be pretty easy to coordinate your breathing. Once you're hugging or spooning, the man matches his breathing pattern to the woman's. For gay couples, larger partners can match their breathing pattern with the smaller partners'. In other words, when the woman (or smaller partner) inhales, the man (or larger partner) inhales simultaneously. When the woman (or smaller partner) exhales, the man (or larger partner) exhales. One partner simply breathes at a normal pace, while the other matches that pace. Continue this coordinated breathing while holding each other for at least three minutes.

Three minutes is the *minimum* amount of time I suggest for the full "magic" of this exercise to work. If you can do it for five minutes, you'll get an even better result. Once you're done, you can decide together what to do next. If you decide to talk about any upset you were experiencing before the exercise, you'll be in a much better place to do so. You can also try using the enhanced listening technique described in chapter 24 after completing your Spoon Tune.

Simple and Easy Practice

When you are upset, the Spoon Tune may be something of a reach. Fortunately, you can still take advantage of the magic of this method in a quicker and more informal way. When stressed, simply get in the habit of asking your partner for a hug. This can be a normal hug (front to front) or more like spooning (front to back). While being hugged, attempt to match your breathing pattern to your partner's. Even thirty seconds of hugging your partner in this manner can make a major difference in how each of you feel.

If even asking for a hug feels awkward, try any type of touch as a way of reducing stress and feeling more connected. Simply hold hands or touch in any way that feels comfortable. My wife and I both love to have our hands massaged, so if we feel stressed, we often take turns trading silent hand massages. The hands (and ears) contain a lot of acupressure points. By massaging them, you literally release a lot of "feel-good" endorphins into your brain. Once you feel better, it becomes much easier to talk about any issues you need to discuss.

CHAPTER 20

Share Your Wisdom

My wife and I are both therapists, so we both enjoy giving advice. Unfortunately, we're not as good at receiving it—especially from each other! That's too bad, because sometimes your mate has a perspective or wisdom that can really be helpful. To counteract the tendency of resisting advice from your partner, I developed an exercise called the Higher Self that allows a couple to step temporarily into the roles of therapist and patient, or guru and student, without resistance. Knowing that the assumption of these roles has a clear endpoint allows couples to share their wisdom without resentment. This can be both an enlightening and a light-hearted means to connect in new ways.

The method is simple. After creating a safe space with no distractions, the couple decides who will assume the role of guru—the Higher Self—and who will play the role of student. The student then presents any situation or problem that is causing stress or upset. (It can even be about the other partner!) Then the Higher Self, or guru, responds with his or her best wisdom and perspective on the matter. Partners can follow up with additional questions, and a natural conversation often continues about the issue at hand until the "troubled" partner feels satisfied and soothed.

A key stipulation when performing this exercise is that those playing the role of the Higher Self must either be blindfolded or have their eyes closed throughout their answer. There are a couple of reasons for this. When we talk to people, we normally look to see if what we're saying is meeting with approval. By having their eyes closed, partners playing the Higher Self can instead simply focus on what they feel is important to say—not on whether it is well received. This allows unfiltered wisdom to flow more easily. Moreover, when we close our eyes, we seem to find it easier to tap into a deeper, wiser part of ourselves. People are often surprised by how much more wise they feel when they answer questions with their eyes closed.

This simple method can have surprising results. Recently, I had people at a workshop pair up with someone they didn't know. One person asked a question and the other person—with eyes closed—responded. Many people were flabbergasted by the answers they received. They couldn't believe that someone who didn't even know them could give them such detailed and helpful answers. Many of those playing the Higher Self were equally surprised. Several reported that they felt as if they were "channeling" some kind of wise being, and they didn't even know what this being was going to say until the words left their mouths. I know this sounds strange, and your results may vary, but you may very well be surprised by this technique.

Recently, my wife and I tried this exercise. She asked my Higher Self how to change something about *me* that she found annoying. While I might normally have gotten defensive about her request, since she was asking my Higher Self the question, I wasn't annoyed at all. In fact, my advice to her was very helpful. She used the advice and found that it did, indeed, work. That's the type of incredible results that can come from this exercise.

The Higher Self

After creating a "container" with no distractions, decide who will play the role of the guru, or Higher Self, and who will present the problem or troubling situation. Make sure that the partner playing the Higher Self is either blindfolded or has his or her eyes closed throughout the exercise. After the student poses the problem, the Higher Self responds with wisdom or perspective on the issue. If either partner feels a need to ask additional questions, they can do so. Let a natural conversation develop about the issue at hand and continue until the "troubled" partner feels satisfied.

Once one partner has received guidance, you can switch roles—or not. You don't have to reverse roles unless both partners agree that is, indeed, what they want to do. Depending on the question and the circumstances, this practice can be done in two minutes or it may take twenty. It may even involve aspects of a "holy ritual"—perhaps having the person playing the Higher Self wear a special outfit. Try hamming it up, especially if it helps both of you get into the spirit of the exercise.

Simple and Easy Practice

If you don't have much time or you want a minimum amount of pretense, you can simply say to your mate: "Can I ask you a question and get your best advice?" If he or she agrees, then proceed to ask your question. If you've done this exercise before, remind your partner about the advantages of closing his or her eyes. When your partner is done giving you advice, express thanks for the wisdom shared—even if you don't agree with it. Couples that can truly take in advice and wisdom from their partners are very fortunate. Two heads are always better than one.

PART IV

Reducing Conflict

Sometimes I wonder how you put up with me. Then I remember, oh, I put up with you, so we're even.

UNKNOWN

To become a master communicator, you must be able to talk things out even when you're upset with someone. Fortunately, this is a skill that you can acquire and hone gradually. Once you have acquired it, you'll be amazed at how much better things go for you and your partner. Trying to have a long-term loving relationship without knowing how to handle upsets is like driving a car with a flat tire. The ride can get very bumpy. The exercises in part 4 will help to smooth out your ride, make it more comfortable, and get you out of dreaded "traffic jams."

Some of the methods presented here can be rather difficult to use. If you and your partner are going through a rough patch, consider doing some of the exercises in the earlier chapters first. The methods presented there can often help partners better understand each other or increase the positive feelings between them.

But we've all been through troubled times when understanding is not enough. We hit a thorny issue or a repetitive pattern that doesn't seem to go away no matter what we do. At those times, the powerful methods given here can help turn difficult conversations into opportunities for healing and growth.

CHAPTER 21

Care for Yourself

When you are upset with your partner, it's easy to fall into the old patterns of fight, flight, or freeze. Ideally, when we are stressed, our mates can give us the care and understanding we need to feel better. Of course, *they* are usually stressed out as well and may not have any care to give. So when you're upset, it's helpful to have a tool that can quickly give *you* the care and support you need to feel more centered. I call this skill "self-empathy."

Self-empathy allows you to feel calm and understood without having to rely on your partner's communication skills. By quickly giving yourself the care and empathy you crave, you can feel better immediately. Once you feel better, your communication with your mate will generally be a lot more effective.

I tell couples that when they are upset or dealing with a thorny issue, the first step is to slow *way* down. When we are stressed, our minds often speed up and get a little crazy. Yet, what we really want—connection—requires plenty of time. The speed with which our minds work can often interfere with the time needed for our hearts to become fully engaged. So the first step to self-empathy is to slow way down. At the very least, take a couple of slow deep breaths. Realize that, if you continue to speak from your emotional upset and plow quickly ahead, a disaster is likely to ensue. If need be, tell your partner you need a minute to simply calm down a little. If you find it helpful, you may even close your eyes for this period of time. By taking a minute to yourself, you will allow your partner to calm down as well.

I can give you an example from my own experience. Recently, my wife and I went camping with some friends. She's not a big fan of camping, so, to some extent, it was I who persuaded her to go on this trip. Well, things weren't going well. Our camping neighbors drank a lot and were generally loud and obnoxious. Then it began to rain, and we had to sit inside our leaking tent for many hours. My wife was very upset; she blamed me for "dragging" her along on this "disastrous trip." I realized her remarks were triggering a negative reaction in me. So I said: "I'd like to better understand the difficulty you're feeling, but I need a minute to myself first." We both sat silently in our water-logged and tension-filled tent. I knew I had limited time, so I got to work on my self-empathy right away.

Sitting there in the tent, I silently said to myself: "This is really, really hard. You came here to have a good time, and now you're both upset and faced with a very challenging situation. I really feel bad for you. I know you tried hard, and it hurts to be disappointed and have your wife be so upset. It's even harder when she blames you. But you'll be okay. You're taking time out for yourself, so you're already doing great. You're not lashing out at her, and that makes me proud of you. Just take some deep breaths, listen to her pain, and soon it will be better. Then you can tell her you really just want more fun and connection with her, and she'll probably soften up. Just stay empathic and caring a little while longer. You can do it."

Although this internal pep talk may sound strange when shared here, this "emergency dose" of self-empathy worked wonders. In about a minute, I went from being angry and hurt to feeling caring and clear about what I needed to do. My wife reacted immediately to my shift in demeanor. She apologized for blaming me, and we had a discussion about what we really wanted from this trip. Soon, we were hugging each other and feeling the connection we were really after all along.

Self-Empathy Pep Talk

Your self-empathy pep talk may sound completely different from mine. Experiment and see what works for you. There are no clear rules as to the "right" way to give yourself empathy. However, there are some helpful guidelines you may want to consider. Try different things and see what works best for you. For me, I find it helpful when I imagine what a loving parent would say to a hurt or upset eight-year-old. I've learned that hearing loving, compassionate words from an imaginary parent quickly helps me feel less hurt and more understood.

It can also be very helpful to have a ritualized "quick practice" to do when you are triggered by your partner—questions like these that were presented in chapter 2:

1. What am I feeling?
2. What am I really wanting?
3. What is my partner feeling, thinking, and wanting?

By answering these questions, you'll be able to return to your conversation with your partner in much better shape than you were in before you took a brief break.

Another quick way to take care of yourself and be more available for your partner is to move your body in beneficial ways. Try stretching, yawning a few times, or simply taking some mindful, slow breaths. The important thing is to find what works best for you and to commit to doing your self-care practice when you need it most.

If you're very upset, and a single minute is not enough to calm you down, ask for more time before engaging in conversation. Once again, use your time wisely. Taking a brisk walk, playing with a pet, listening to music, or even watching funny YouTube clips are all powerful acts of self-care. The important thing is to find what works for you and remember to use it the next time you feel blamed, misunderstood, or upset.

Simple and Easy Practice

Think back to a recent time when you were really upset with your partner. Write out exactly what you would have *wanted* them—or a loving parent—to say to you in that moment to make you feel better. Then, the next time you find yourself in a comparable situation, say similar words to yourself during a brief pause in the conversation. Notice how that affects what happens next. I think you'll be pleased.

Another simple and easy practice is to make a list of three quick self-care activities you can do to feel better immediately. Preferably, these activities should be things that don't cost much money, are easily accessible, and are in no way harmful to your mind or body. There are many ways to do this. Your task is to find out what works best for you.

CHAPTER 22

Show Empathy

In my opinion, the single most important thing you can do to improve your relationship is to better understand your partner. Understanding involves two key skills: you must *understand* the feelings your partner has about a given situation, and you must *express* that understanding in a way that he or she can appreciate. Understanding and valuing your partner's perspective leads to empathy. And the more empathic couples are, the more loving they are likely to be.

Fortunately, understanding your partner's perspective is not the same as agreeing with it. It simply means that his or her perspective makes sense to you and you understand why your partner feels that way. I've developed an exercise that couples can use, not only to understand each other but also to empathize with each other in a way they can both truly appreciate. I call it the "What I heard . . ." exercise, and I think it's the single most important exercise offered in this book.

Most couples spend very little (if any) time trying to truly understand each other—especially when a discussion gets heated. Instead, they try to convince each other how wrong the other's perspective is, or they simply blame them for the whole problem.

These behaviors are a complete waste of time and energy. As I said in chapter 1, people don't care what you have to say until they feel that you care. The way to demonstrate that you care is to listen, empathize, and show that you understand someone's point of view—even if you don't agree with it. Unfortunately, this is very hard to do when emotions are running high. The "What I heard . . ." exercise can help you reach a place of empathy and understanding even when you'd rather strangle each other.

Let's look at how Jane and Joe used this exercise. First, I'll summarize the process and then we'll follow them through the steps:

1. Jane shares something with Joe that is weighing on her mind or heart. It can be about anything. She can share for up to two minutes (using a timer is optional).

2. Joe responds by sharing, in abbreviated form, what he heard Jane say. His job is to avoid interpretation as much as possible and to correctly identify the feelings Jane is experiencing.

3. Jane then clarifies and expands on her initial concerns, and clears up any mistaken notions Joe may have voiced in his summary.

4. Joe shares what he felt listening to the whole process and/or what he learned about Jane from her sharing.

Jane and Joe then reverse roles and begin again. Once they have each had a turn to share, they conclude the exercise and move on to something else. I recommend not talking about what was shared for at least an hour, because if you immediately engage in a conversation about what was shared, it may descend into blaming or trying to persuade your partner to see things your way. This can nullify any good feelings of connection you gained from the exercise. Of course, this is just a suggestion. If you feel strongly that you can continue to show empathy during a conversation about what was discussed, give it a try.

Here's an example of Jane and Joe using the exercise:

Jane: *I've been really upset about* how you don't seem to be doing any of the housework around here. We both are working a lot, but it seems that I'm the one always doing the dishes, cleaning up after you, and doing the laundry. Sometimes, I feel as if I'm your maid. And I don't think you even notice all the stuff I do. It's as if it's invisible to you. In fact, sometimes you seem irritated that I'm doing all these things to keep the house clean. Well, I like a clean house. I'm not like you; I'm not okay if things are lying around. I'd like you to respect that.

Joe: *What I heard you say is* you're upset that you're doing all the chores, and that you'd like me to put in my fair share of work around the house. I also heard you say that you need a clean house, because it makes you feel better.

Jane: *I would also add* that I don't feel appreciated for all that I'm doing. I feel that you take everything I do for granted—and I resent that.

Joe: *What I got from your sharing is* you feel resentful and not appreciated for all the work you're doing. I learned that you really value a clean house, and you at least want to be appreciated when you work to keep it clean.

It helps to use the specific sentence prompts given in italics to keep the conversation moving in the right direction.

The structure of this exercise may seem clumsy at first. But it's intended to increase the chances that true empathic listening is likely to occur. Its main purpose is to help partners really understand the emotions their mates are experiencing. If you simply mimic your partner's words without any sense that you understand the feelings his or her story evokes, you won't be tapping into the full power of this method. When partners feel that they understand each other's stories *and* their feelings, then miracles happen. Emotional walls that have been built up over years can come tumbling down in seconds.

What I Heard . . .

The sequence for this exercise is very specific and must be followed quite precisely. If you veer from it, you will likely end up blaming your partner and escalating whatever problem you have between the two of you.

Begin by sitting together and deciding who will go first. Decide how long each partner will speak, then complete these four sentence prompts. You can use a timer if you like.

1. Partner #1: What's been going on with me is . . . (tell your story).
2. Partner #2: What I heard you say is . . . (summarize what you heard).
3. Partner #1: I would also like to add . . . (clarify anything that was missed during the recap).
4. Partner #2: What I got from your sharing is . . . (summarize the most important thing you learned).

This exercise and the simple practice below may not sound like much. But the skill of providing empathic understanding is the single most important ability you need to be a master communicator. When partners really feel that they understand each other and feel each other's pain, it encourages them to relax. It allows them to let go of the stress they've been holding on to. It helps them to feel better immediately. Once that happens, you'll find that you are more available to listen to each other—and to understand each other's feelings. My clients are often flabbergasted by how well these tools work. You'll be pleasantly surprised, too—if you use them. So don't delay. Start today.

Simple and Easy Practice

You can be empathic at any time. Here is a simple and easy way to get you moving in the right direction whenever your partner tells you about something that is causing difficulty or frustration. In response to hearing your partner's story, say: "It sounds like . . ." Then, in one sentence or less, summarize what you heard. Then add: "That must feel (or must have felt) . . . " (identify how you think your partner feels). For instance, in response to your partner complaining about work, you could say: "It sounds like you had a really difficult day. That must feel really frustrating."

Of course, you don't have to stick to these exact words. Feel free to use whatever empathic words feel most natural to you. And avoid trying to fix your partner's problem until *after* you provide some empathy. In fact, once you show your partner some empathy, you may not need to fix the problem at all. In many cases, the problem was really that your partner just needed some empathy!

CHAPTER 23

Take Responsibility

Taking responsibility is actually quite hard to do. We often see others' mistakes much more clearly than our own. Moreover, taking responsibility makes us feel vulnerable, and true vulnerability is not easy to bear. When you and your partner are experiencing difficulties, however, it can have a major impact if you can really acknowledge the ways in which you have contributed to the problem at hand. The ability to take responsibility can take your relationship to a whole new level of maturity, love, and harmony. And it's a surefire way to end arguments and relieve feelings of separation.

When couples are having a hard time, they want their partners to understand them. By taking responsibility for how their behavior is contributing to the problem at hand, partners can indirectly show each other that they *do* understand the other's point of view. Once partners feel understood, they can magically let go of blame—since they no longer have to *convince* each other to see their individual perspectives. When both partners are willing to take responsibility, it can stop a fight in its tracks. Here's an example of how taking responsibility really helped to defuse a conflict.

Joseph and Jerry were in my office debating about who was to blame for the problems they were having. Jerry accused Joseph of "nonstop complaining." Meanwhile, Joseph felt justified in yelling at Jerry for his remarks. Both of them were presenting evidence about how the other was in the wrong—and each of them wanted me to act as a judge and pronounce one innocent and the other guilty. Instead, I suggested they try a quick exercise to shed some light on the situation.

First, I asked them each to answer the question: "How has my behavior contributed to the problem at hand?" As often happens, they both drew a blank when faced with this possibility. Had I asked: "How is your *partner* contributing to the problem at hand?" I would probably have gotten an hour-long lecture from each of them—complete with precise examples, quotes, and eye-witness accounts. Knowing how hard it is for people to come up with how they are specifically responsible for something, I had two other questions ready to help them unearth their previously hidden contributions to the problem under discussion: "How have any of my shortcomings made this more difficult for my partner?" and "Have I said or done something, or not said or not done something, that has contributed to this problem?" Here's how Jerry and Joseph responded:

Me: Jerry, why don't you start by telling us a specific way in which you have contributed to the upset going on?

Jerry: I know I can be very stubborn—especially when I'm upset, and I'm sure that's no fun to deal with.

Me: Good. Joseph, your turn.

Joseph: I guess I got lost in my self-righteousness again. I have been making excuses for being late again.

Then I asked each of them to search their hearts for any specific behavior they regretted having done and, if it felt right, apologize for it. I asked them to answer the question: "How have any of my shortcomings made this more difficult for my partner?"

> **Jerry:** I can see how I made you even more upset when I told you I can't stand how you're complaining all the time. I sometimes say mean things when I'm upset. I apologize for that.

> **Joseph:** Thank you for saying that. I recognize I started shouting at you the other day, and I realize I have an anger problem. I'm sorry you have to deal with that. I wish it were different.

Now there was a totally different energy between Jerry and Joseph than there had been a couple of minutes before. Joseph held out his hand to Jerry, and Jerry tenderly embraced it. I felt grateful for being able to watch this moment of emotional healing.

How Did I Contribute?

Whenever you sense that a conversation is veering into an argument or is filled with blame, try the following exercise. It involves each partner asking him or herself three questions to identify specific ways they may have contributed to the problem at hand. I call it the "How did I contribute?" exercise, because it requires partners to reveal how their *specific* words or actions contributed to a *specific* conflict. It is not effective merely to say: "Ultimately I'm responsible for our relationship." Statements like that are too general to have an impact. The impact of this exercise comes from pinpointing the exact way in which you are responsible in the specific situation you're currently dealing with.

This exercise is so powerful that you generally only need to do one round to break the momentum of an argument, but taking turns sharing through two or even three rounds is even better:

1. Ask yourself: "How has my behavior contributed to the problem at hand?" If, like most people, you have difficulty answering this more general question in a specific way, move on to the second question.

2. Ask yourself: "How have any of my shortcomings made this more difficult for my partner?" Make sure that your responses are specific and detailed. And make sure that they address the particular problem you are facing at the moment, not just general feelings of discontent or frustration. Share your answers with your partner.

3. Ask yourself: "Have I said or done something, or not said or not done something, that has contributed to this problem?" Again, be specific and answer in the context of the present problem. What exactly did you do? What exactly did you say? What exactly did you fail to do or say? What could you have said or done? Share these answers with your partner.

While apologizing for your behavior isn't necessary, it does tend to increase the impact of what you say. Don't try to fake remorse, however. That does no one any good. But if you really *are* sorry for how you acted, why not say so? Apologizing is hard on the ego, which is why most people don't do it. None of us wants to admit that we are ever wrong. But would you rather be right and self-righteous—or would you rather be loved by your partner? You choose. You can rarely have both.

Don't wait until you're screaming at each other to use this exercise. In fact, it's best to learn and practice this method when things aren't so heated. If you have a few practice rounds under your belt while dealing with small problems, when a real crisis hits, you'll be prepared for it. This technique works amazingly well and can quickly turn a nasty interaction in a positive new direction. Unfortunately, there is generally a lot of resistance to doing it *because* it works so well. But if you've read this far, you're both persistent and brave. You're up for the challenge.

Simple and Easy Practice

Since taking responsibility is a skill that gets better with practice, consider doing it by yourself during the day, anytime there's a problem in your life. The three questions in the exercise above can point you in the right direction and help you see ways in which you are partly—but specifically—responsible for difficulties in your life. Simply complete the following sentence: "I can see that my (specific behavior/shortcoming) contributed to (the problem at hand.)" For example: "I can see that my tendency to rush and leave late contributed to our being late to the party tonight." Try to be precise in stating what you feel you did poorly. If your partner is available and you feel it appropriate, you can share your answer. If you feel regretful for this behavior, tell your partner that as well. Then notice how your partner's tone changes. In most cases, unless your partner has a lot of stored up resentments, he or she will relax—and may even take some responsibility for the problem as well. Halleluiah!

CHAPTER 24

Speak Your Heart

In my communication workshops, I have partners do a paired "listening exercise" in which one partner speaks about his or her hopes for the future while the other listens. I have the speaking partners briefly close their eyes while, on the white board, I write a "secret technique" for the listening partners to use. What I write on the board are the following words: Listen intensely to your partner for twenty seconds, then become *increasingly distracted*. Then, I erase the "secret technique" and tell the speakers they can open their eyes. The speaking partners proceed to talk about their hopes for the future. By the time two minutes have passed, most listeners are looking at their phones, glancing away, playing with their pens, etc. Meanwhile, most talkers are so upset by this that they either stop talking completely or start insulting their listening partners. It's a bit funny and a bit tragic to watch.

Once this train wreck of an exercise is over, I ask participants what they learned from it. The main thing they learn is how hard it is to talk to someone who isn't giving you his or her full attention. They start to see that communication is a dance between two people. If the person doing the listening is distracted, the person doing the talking tends to shut down the exchange.

Studies on the length of the human attention span carried out by Microsoft Corporation have shown that the average person's attention span has dropped from twelve seconds to less than eight seconds over the past two decades. To put that in perspective, goldfish are believed to have an attention span of nine seconds! Due to what I call WMDs—Widgets of Mass Distraction—human beings are losing their ability to focus on anything for very long. People get bored more easily than in times past, and their ability to listen to other people is becoming weaker. This shortening attention span does not bode well for couples trying to understand each other.

Another obstacle that interferes with our ability to listen to each other is our increasing tendency to interrupt. It used to be that interrupting someone was considered rather rude. Unfortunately, however, it is becoming more and more prevalent and acceptable in our ADHD society, partly due to the fact that our smartphones are constantly interrupting us with texts, alerts, and calls. But interruptions are never appreciated in good communication. When you interrupt someone, you basically give them the following message: "What you have to say is so boring or so predictable that I'm going to stop you right now and save a few seconds of my precious time so I can tell you what's really important." If someone actually said those words to you, you'd likely consider them rude and boorish. But that's basically what you are saying (nonverbally) when you interrupt your partner.

To remedy our decreasing attention spans and our increasing tendency to interrupt, I developed the following exercise. Try it and see if it helps to make your communications with your partner more effective and supportive.

You Talk . . . I'll Listen

In this technique, partners take turns speaking without any interruptions for a specified length of time—typically three, four, or five minutes. While one partner speaks, the other's job is to listen as best he or she can, making a conscious effort to avoid distractions and interruptions. Once the first person is done, the partners trade roles. Very simple. Afterward, you can choose to comment on what each other said, or you can choose to avoid comment. Whatever works best.

I know this method doesn't sound like much, and maybe it won't be a magical technique for you and your mate. However, many couples find it both powerful and beneficial. When we know we won't be interrupted and we have some time to speak, it changes what we talk about. People tend to get below the surface of life and really reveal what they are experiencing. Meanwhile, because the listening partner knows there will be no chance to respond, he or she can simply listen. Often, this listening deepens to the point of true empathic understanding. This kind of connected communication is healing for both partners.

If you find yourself having a hard time knowing what to say in your three-to-five minute monologue, here are some sentence prompts that may help you get started:

1. What's been going on with me lately is . . .

2. Something I've been seeing or learning in my life is . . .

3. In our relationship, I've been noticing . . .

4. Lately, I've been concerned about . . .

5. Lately, I've been hoping . . .

Try the prompts if they feel right to you, or feel free to make up your own. While you may feel awkward using this method at first, that discomfort will likely soon fade as you start talking. Think of this practice as a way for you and your partner to explore your life and your relationship comfortably. You never know what will be revealed, but my experience shows that this exercise often leads to a deeper connection between partners. I have found it can be particularly helpful when partners are hesitant to talk much about their feelings or tend to flee or freeze when stressed. Having a designated time to speak openly can give these people full permission to explore their feelings.

A good place to do this exercise is in your car with your partner. As long as you're not in a rush, a car can be a place that's conducive to fewer distractions and deeper communication. Say something like: "Is it okay if I talk for a few minutes about what I've been thinking lately?" Once you get a "green light" from your partner, begin. If, after you're done talking, it feels appropriate, ask your partner to talk about what's been going on in his or her life.

When we really listen to our partners, we give them a gift. We make it much easier for them to dive into their hearts and explore what's really there. This exercise can also help couples strengthen their ability to listen to each other. Hopefully, once that ability is strengthened, it will play an increasing role in your daily interactions. When two people can really listen to each other, every part of their relationship is enhanced.

Simple and Easy Practice

To practice better listening, you need not set up a special exercise. You can simply ask a question and listen to your partner's response without interruption. It's amazing how intimacy can grow and how much you can learn by simply listening. If you find that talking for several minutes is hard for you to do, try writing a letter detailing what you're feeling or what you've been experiencing. When you're done, exchange letters (or emails) with your partner.

CHAPTER 25

Tell the Truth

A slow-growing type of "cancer" can often take hold in long-term partnerships. Slowly but surely, a pattern of suppressing certain thoughts, feelings, and behaviors grows. By themselves, each of these "suppressions" may not seem like a big deal. But as they accumulate, they create—as Pink Floyd would say—another brick in the wall. This "wall" of suppression can soon become impenetrable, and true intimacy becomes almost impossible.

Why do people withhold information in intimate relationships? Basically, it's because they don't feel safe enough to reveal the full truth of who they are. Most likely, they have tried to be honest in the past, and the "reward" they received was an earful of condemnation. Overcoming this pattern requires structured communication in which disapproving feedback is eliminated and couples can begin to tear down this wall. The "Would you like to hear . . . ?" exercise provides for this kind of exchange by delaying any response or feedback for twenty-four hours. This creates a safe "space" in which partners can honestly reveal any "bricks" in the wall of suppression they've created.

When tearing down a wall, it's important to do it carefully. Any reckless or impulsive behavior can easily lead to disaster. After all, you don't want the wall to come tumbling down on your head. Unfortunately, many couples spend years slowly building a wall of suppression and, when they can't stand it anymore, try to blow it up all at once and hope for the best. This rarely goes well—especially in cases where a safe container has not been adequately established. When revealing withheld information, establishing a safe space is the key to success.

Establishing a safe place for honest communication requires attention and care. The process consists of partners sharing information in a precise sequence that helps to make them both feel safe. And there are two very important rules that are critical to the success of this technique:

- Partners *must not* discuss any material revealed for at least twenty-four hours.
- The material revealed in the exercise *must* be held as sacred.

It is not easy to reveal information that has been suppresssed or witheld, so you have to give those revelations the space and respect they deserve.

Here's an example of how this exercise helped save a relationship. By the time Valerie and Kevin entered my office, it was obvious that a wall the size of the Great Wall of China had been built between them. They didn't look at each other, and they didn't really even know what was wrong. Their complaint was that they hadn't had sex in over a year. No wonder. It looked as if neither of them had smiled in over a year either. I suggested they try three rounds of the "Would you like to hear . . . ?" exercise. Here's what happened:

Me: Valerie, why don't you start.

Valerie: There's something I've been withholding. Would you like to hear it?

Kevin: Yes, I'd like to hear it.

Valerie: Your breath smells really bad in the morning. It makes me not want to kiss you or be next to you.

Kevin: Thank you. I have something I've been withholding, too. Would you like to hear it?

Valerie: Yes, I'd like to hear it.

Kevin: I've been flirting with a woman at the office. We haven't done anything, but I certainly have wanted to. She's married, too, and I think that's what has stopped us from having an affair.

Valerie: Why didn't you tell me about this before? This is why I don't trust you!

I warned Valerie that she was not allowed to talk about or make comments on what Kevin said for a full twenty-four hours. I advised her to take a couple of deep breaths and say: "Thank you."

Valerie (after some deep breaths): Thank you. I have something I've been withholding. Would you like to hear it?

Kevin: Yes, I'd like to hear it.

Valerie: Lately, I've been feeling really hopeless about our marriage. I'm too afraid to get a divorce, but I'm too unhappy to continue to live like this—like roommates.

Kevin: Thank you. (He takes a couple of deep breaths.) I have something I've been withholding. Would you like to hear it?

Valerie: Yes, I'd like to hear it.

Kevin: Since we basically don't have any sex life, I've been watching a lot of porn. I've basically given up on our sex life because you are never in the mood. Now I'm not in the mood either. I'd rather watch porn.

Valerie: Thank you.

For the final round, I asked them to try sharing something tender or positive.

Valerie: I have something I've been withholding. Would you like to hear it?

Kevin: Yes, I'd like to hear it.

Valerie: I really miss you. I'm scared you'll have an affair and leave me. I feel really sad that we barely talk now—and I don't know what to do. I miss hearing your laugh, and I miss cuddling with you. I miss the good times we used to have.

Kevin (his eyes filling with tears): Thank you. I have something I've been withholding. Would you like to hear it?

Valerie: Yes, I'd like to hear it.

Kevin: I love your smell and the way you used to kiss me all over. And I love your smile. Your whole face lights up. It makes me really happy to see you happy.

Valerie: Thank you.

As you can see, this exercise can get pretty intense. It can even stir up issues you've been wanting to avoid. If you provide a safe place for these communications and guarantee the sanctity of their content, this kind of sharing can quickly lead to the trust and intimacy you desire.

Would You Like to Hear . . . ?

The rules of this method must be followed quite precisely. Remember to follow the sequence as given, and above all, remember to withold comment for twenty-fours and to respect the sanctity of the information revealed. Here are the steps. I suggest that you review them together before you start so you can both feel safe while doing the exercise.

1. Establish a set amount of time or a set number of rounds for the exercise. If you decide on an amount of time, set a timer.
2. Set aside a quiet place with no distractions.
3. Clearly state your intention to feel more connected and to remove any obstacles to honesty and intimacy.
4. Begin with the first partner saying: "There's something I've been withholding. Would you like to hear it?"
5. The second partner responds: "Yes, I'd like to hear it."
6. The first partner shares whatever he or she has been withholding.
7. The second partner responds by simply saying: "Thank you." Remember, make no other response for at least twenty-four hours.
8. Reverse roles and repeat steps 4 through 7.

This ends one full round. Continue until you have completed the number of rounds agreed upon or until you have used the amount of time specified. Remember that it can be helpful to use the last round to reveal something that is supportive in nature so the exercise ends on a positive note. At the risk of being redundant, I want to repeat the two absolutely critical rules of this exercise:

- No comment on information revealed is allowed for at least twenty-four hours.
- Information revealed is to be held as sacred.

Remember that it is not easy to reveal withheld information, so give it the space and respect it deserves. This not only helps to create a safe container for the exercise; it also helps teach you important skills for creating safety *outside* the context of the technique. Like training wheels on a bike, allowing honesty without immediate feedback can teach you to keep from falling into patterns that hurt.

Here are a couple of extra tips that can help you be successful when using this exercise. First, stick to the script. While the formality of the technique may seem weird at first, the ritualized aspect of the words can help to create a safe space for total honesty. Second, it's helpful to do something fun—or, at the very least, distracting—immediately afterward. Watch a TV show or movie while holding hands or go out for pizza. You've just successfully done "surgery" on your relationship. You deserve a lighthearted reward. This can also help you avoid obsessing about any information that was particularly hard to hear. On the other hand, if you were severely triggered by something your partner said, gently tell them: "Thank you for the exercise and your honesty. I'd like to spend some time by myself for now."

One last piece of advice. This exercise becomes easier the more frequently you do it. Try doing it once every month or two to clear out the accumulated cobwebs in your relationship. For example, try two or three rounds on the first day of each month. I predict you'll soon notice that any wall you've erected will begin to develop spaces where love and light can come shining through.

Simple and Easy Practice

It's best to reveal withheld information spontaneously when you and your partner are feeling happy and/or connected. You can simply begin by telling your partner: "Honey, there's something I haven't told you that I think would be important for you to know. Is now an okay time to tell you?" Your partner will almost certainly agree. After you reveal what you've withheld, be compassionate and empathic when your partner reacts. Later, if it seems appropriate, you can ask: "Is there anything you've not communicated to me that you'd like to share as well?"

Sharing withheld information in a spontaneous manner can be a bit risky because the clear rules that govern the formal exercise have not been established. But it's better than nothing. Just be prepared for some reaction from your partner if what you have to say is particularly hard to hear. Revealing withheld information is hard work. The good news is that, while walls get built slowly over time, they can be taken down rather quickly. All you need is the right method and the right intention.

CHAPTER 26

Work Together

When couples have difficulties in their intimate relationship, the "problem" is rarely the problem. More often than not, there are two other challenges in play: both partners probably feel as if they are not truly understood by the other, and both partners probably feel threatened by the problem at hand. We tend to deal with problems and conflict in the reptilian part of our brains—we fight, we flee, or we freeze. When we sit down and rationally analyze how best to overcome a problem, however, we often find that the answer is simple. That's why the exercise in this chapter can come to the rescue. I call it Searching for Solutions.

This exercise can help couples get on the same page when dealing with troubling issues or persistent conflict. Instead of focusing on blame, it focuses on workable solutions to the issues at hand. With a common goal in mind and a spirit of cooperation, creative and practical solutions are almost guaranteed to emerge.

The trickiest part of this exercise is often coming to agreement on just what the "problem" is. Your mate may say: "You don't listen to me." But you may say: "I *do* listen, but you don't get that I'm hearing and understanding you." Who is right? Both of you are. But arguing over whose problem it is does not get you any closer to a solution. Instead, you may need to step back and state the problem in a more general manner. For example, try saying: "We have a problem in which both of us feel as if the other doesn't really understand."

Coming up with a statement about the problem that you both agree on can be challenging—but it's necessary. You can't solve something that's undefined or something that you each define in different ways. This exercise can make your job easier by helping you come up with a mutually satisfying statement of just what the problem is.

Unlike other methods in this book, this one is very much based on rational deliberation not emotions or feelings. If you feel that you first need your partner to understand you better before searching for solutions to a problem, try using the "Would you like to hear . . . ?" exercise in chapter 25 before proceeding with this technique.

This exercise succeeds through the simple process of identifying, prioritizing, and analyzing possible solutions to the problem at hand. Partners identify at least three specific ways to handle a problem, put them in order of preference, and share them with each other. They then rate each other's solutions on a scale of 1 to 10 (with 1 being least acceptable and 10 being most acceptable) and find which ones are the most agreeable to them both. If no solutions are agreeable to both, they try to negotiate a solution. Mark and Emily used it to deal with an issue regarding a lack of money and lack of quality time spent together. First, they agreed on the nature of the problem, then they used the structure of the exercise to come up with various solutions to solve it:

Mark: So how would you define the problem at hand?

Emily: I'd say we're not spending enough quality time together.

Mark: I agree with that, but I think there's more to it. I think the problem is we're both working a lot and are too tired to spend quality time together.

Emily: And then there's the issue of not having money to pay for babysitters or take a vacation together.

Mark: So the problem is that we don't spend much time together because we're working a lot and what extra energy we do have is spent on the kids.

Emily: Okay, I agree. So why don't we define the problem as: We don't spend enough time together because we work a lot, and we don't have extra money to spend on babysitters.

Mark: That works for me.

They wrote down the problem as stated and then each wrote down three specific solutions and put them in order—1 for most preferred; 3 for least preferred. Mark began the sharing process.

Mark: My #1 solution is to put off taking a vacation for another year until we have more money and can afford to hire a babysitter for more than a few hours.

Emily: I rate that solution as a 2 on a scale of 1 to 10.

Mark: My #2 solution is to have a date night once a week and have a friend of ours babysit. In exchange, we can babysit their kids once a week.

Emily: I rate that solution as a 7.

Mark: My #3 solution is to have a date night or a weekend together and pay for the babysitter by putting more things on our credit cards.

Emily: I rate that as a 5.

Emily then shared her solutions.

Emily: My #1 solution is to work fewer hours and, with my extra time, create fun things to do together and hire a babysitter so we can go out more. We'll simply keep fixing the old car instead of trying to buy a new one so we can pay for babysitters.

Mark: I rate that as a 3.

Emily: My #2 solution is to find a friend who is willing to babysit the kids, and we can take turns babysitting their kids.

Mark: I rate that as an 8.

Emily: My #3 solution is for you to spend less on gadgets and for me to spend less on clothes, and with the extra money hire a babysitter and have a nice date night each week.

Mark: I rate that as a 7.

Mark and Emily eventually decided to implement two of their solutions. They agreed to spend less money on gadgets and clothes for a month and also to ask a friend with kids to trade babysitting duties once a week. With the money they saved from buying less, they opened an account to save for a one-week vacation. These solutions ended up working for them. Had they not, they could have explored other options.

This exercise works for three main reasons. First, it focuses on finding solutions, rather than on assigning blame. Second, it forces you to come up with *several* solutions. This keeps you from digging in on your own favorite option. Finally, it gives each partner feedback on how the other is reacting to their ideas. Rather than just getting a simple "yes" or "no" to their suggestions, partners learn exactly how *much* they like or dislike each other's ideas.

This exercise is no magic bullet. It's still hard to work out mutually satisfying solutions. After all, if it were easy, your problem would already be solved. But this structured approach can provide you with all the information you need to come up with the best possible solution.

Searching for Solutions

To begin, set aside some time and find a quiet place where you won't be interrupted. The exercise works best if you write your solutions down, so have paper and pens or pencils handy.

1. Agree upon a clear statement of the problem. This may take several rounds of suggestions and modifications. Just go about it carefully and methodically. The wording you come up with will be important to arriving at solutions you agree on.

2. Once you have agreed upon a clear statement of the problem at hand, each partner writes down at least three specific ways to solve it.

3. Put the solutions in order, with 1 being the most preferred solution, and 3 being the least preferred.

4. Tell your partner your #1 solution and have him or her rate it on a scale of 1 to 10, with 1 being least acceptable and 10 being most acceptable. Make a note of your partner's rating next to the solution.

5. Repeat this for your second and third solutions, keeping track of how your partner rates them.

6. When you are finished, reverse roles and repeat steps 2 through 5.

7. Once you have both shared and rated all your solutions, identify the solutions that are rated the highest (closest to 10) and discuss the solutions that seem most agreeable to both of you.

If no solutions seem particularly agreeable to you both, negotiate a solution by asking each other the question: "What would it take to make my most agreeable solution worth a try to you?" At this point, you're really in a negotiation with your partner, which is certainly a whole lot better than a shouting match. If you and your partner still feel stuck, try coming up with a very short-term solution. For instance, you may be willing to commit to buying fewer clothes or gadgets for a year to pay for babysitters, but your partner may only be willing to do that for a month. If you try it for a month and it seems to be working pretty well, try it for another month. If it doesn't work out well, try something else.

This exercise works because it forces you to stay focused on solutions and relevant information, rather than getting lost in irrelevant issues and obstacles. If you can do that with your mate, you may be surprised at how often you end up solving your problems amicably.

Simple and Easy Practice

If you find that you are starting to disagree over some issue, but you don't think your partner would be agreeable to a structured exercise, try asking this simple question: "What are two or three ideas you have for how we might be able to handle this issue effectively?" Then wait to hear what he or she has to say. If you like one of the ideas, congratulations—you're done. If you don't like *any* of your partner's suggestions, try asking: "Would you be willing to hear a couple of ideas I have for how we might deal with this?" Since you listened first, your partner will surely listen to you. Once all the ideas are out, try to come up with some solution or compromise—even if it's only short-term—that's agreeable to both of you. Or you can just try coming up with three solutions by yourself and presenting them to your mate for reaction. Once multiple solutions are "on the table," it's much easier to come up with some compromise that works for both of you.

CHAPTER 27

Negotiate Change

Changing something about yourself is hard. That's why we rarely do it—even when we know we *should* change and we're highly motivated. For instance, people who smoke cigarettes know they should stop; they even know they're killing themselves—but alas, change is hard. It's even harder when you're okay with your behavior, but your *partner* wants you to change. That makes it doubly hard.

I often hear: "If my partner really loved me, he'd *want* to change." Or: "She shouldn't need me to bribe her in order to change." My response to this is: "If you really loved your partner, *you'd* change and accept your partner just as he or she is." Now, I understand that your partner may be doing something that is clearly self-destructive—like smoking or taking dangerous drugs. But, even in these cases, you're asking your partner to do something huge—and a little extra love and effort from you certainly can't hurt.

That's why I developed the "If you'll . . . Then I'll . . ." exercise to help motivate you or your partner to do the hard work of change. The method is based on a simple principle: If you ask someone to make a major effort for you, you need to make it worthwhile. This exercise can help you negotiate change without falling into the "blaming and shaming" game.

There are four simple guidelines for this technique:

1. Avoid blaming and shaming.
2. Ask for a change in a specific behavior not a general change in character.
3. Offer something in return for your partner committing to a change.
4. Write out the terms of your agreement so they are clear.

Each couple has to discover their own path through these principles. Here's how Carrie and Brad did it.

Carrie and Brad were thinking of getting married, but Carrie was worried about Brad's frequent drinking. At first, Carrie tried pleading with Brad, then shaming him, then blaming him for being an alcoholic. This had the effect of creating distance between them and caused Brad to dig in his heels. I suggested Carrie stop the blaming and shaming and ask instead for the *minimum change* she needed from Brad in order to stay in the relationship.

Previously, Carrie had told Brad that he needed to give up drinking and join AA, but he refused. As she thought about the minimum change she needed, she realized that it was substantially different from this larger, more daunting request. She finally said: "I want him *never* to drive when he's had more than one drink. And I want him never to have more than two drinks a night when he's with me. And I want him never to have more than four beers in a given day."

After Carrie made her request, I asked Brad about his reaction. He said: "That might be doable. But what do I get out of this? That won't be easy." I told him: "That's a fair question. Well, the first thing you get is Carrie. It sounds as if, if you can't commit to that, she's out of here. Another thing you get is her respect and admiration. But if you want something more for this commitment, ask for it."

Brad was silent for about two minutes while Carrie and I waited in anticipation. Finally, he said: "If I'm going to commit to this, I want Carrie to stop complaining about my friends when I invite them over to watch football." Carrie immediately erupted in anger: "Your friends are loud and obnoxious and they mess up the whole house." I interrupted Carrie and said: "Brad put a good faith offer on the table. You asked him to do something that's hard for him, and he's making a similar request of you. Both of you want the other to change a specific behavior that you find objectionable. If you don't like his proposal, do you have a counteroffer?"

After a little bit of negotiation, they agreed to the terms of a deal. Carrie agreed to stop complaining about Brad's friends—as long as he cleaned up after them. Brad agreed to Carrie's suggested limits on alcohol consumption—with the penalty for any violations being a couple of AA meetings.

Some people think negotiations like this are too calculated. They argue that couples should do things out of love. I agree that doing things out of love is good, but the truth is that we're just apes with bigger brains, not saints. We generally make changes only when we see how it clearly benefits us. Negotiations like this really go on all the time—only in a less explicit manner. The "If you'll . . . Then I'll . . ." exercise just makes what would normally be a hidden negotiation very visible. The advantage is that each partner knows the score, and each can now be held accountable to the other.

If You'll . . . Then I'll . . .

Performing this exercise is really as simple as adhering to the four guidelines given above.

- *Avoid blaming and shaming:* Instead, offer caring support for the change you want to see. Change is most likely to occur if blame and shame are absent and caring support is offered instead. This may seem like common sense, but it's not common practice. If couples took half the time they spend on blaming each other and put it toward working out a plan for change, there would be a lot of healthy change going on.

- *Ask for a change in a specific behavior:* Don't ask for a general change of character, like being lazy or stubborn. Only targeted behavioral changes can be negotiated. If you ask your partner to "stop being angry all the time," you just ask for failure. If you ask instead that your partner not yell at you when the kids are home, you may succeed at changing that specific behavior—and that is a good start. The more specific the change you request, the more likely it will happen. Make sure that what you are requesting targets a precise behavior. Smoking, yelling, and leaving dishes in the sink are all behaviors. On the other hand, being stubborn or lazy or uncaring are characteristics based in judgment, not behaviors. Make sure your request is based on a behavior and not a judgment.

- *Offer something in return for your partner committing to a change:* Be willing to do something in return for your partner's efforts. This can be a reward or a commitment to change one of your own specific behaviors. It may be something physical, like buying a wanted item or going on a vacation trip. In the example above, Carrie committed to a stop complaining about Brad's friends coming over to watch football. Whatever you can both agree on is fine—as long as it doesn't hurt anybody.

- *Write down the terms of your agreement so they are clear:* Consider it a contract between the two of you, complete with spelled-out consequences for violations. Both partners should keep a copy of the agreement. Writing your agreements down helps make them binding and can also help you remember what you agreed to.

Negotiating a change with your partner is a skill you can improve with practice. Even if your first attempts feel clumsy, it will likely be better than having no guiding agreements between you. If you need to, get some outside help. Negotiating change can be a tricky business. Sometimes a counselor or mediator can help.

People often get defensive when they're asked to change, so be careful, kind, and empathetic when asking for what you want. Whenever possible, start off with something small—like leaving dishes in the sink. If the change is small enough, the negotiating process can even be fun. Then, if you ever have to deal with bigger issues, like addiction or some other major problem, you'll have some experience in how to create a mutually satisfying agreement. When done right, negotiating a change with your partner can help build trust between you and prevent a lot of future problems.

Simple and Easy Practice

You can use this technique in informal settings without the structure of the larger exercise. Just approach your partner in a nonthreatening way and say something like: "I have a request I'd like you to consider. It would make me feel really wonderful if you could . . . (describe the *specific* change you want in a single sentence). I know it's asking a lot, and I'll still love you if you don't, but this change would make me very happy." Then listen empathetically to any objections your partner has and, if appropriate, offer something you'd be willing to do in exchange.

Another simple and easy practice is to ask yourself: "What one simple change would my partner most want from *me*?" Then, at least for a few days, make that change without telling your partner what you're doing. Once your partner notices something shifting in you, he or she will probably be more agreeable to whatever change you request in return.

CHAPTER 28

Apologize Sincerely

In the world of business, money is the grease that makes everything run smoothly. If all forms of currency (cash, credit cards, checks, etc.) suddenly disappeared, there would be chaos in the business world. In the world of relationships, *trust* is the main form of currency. When trust is betrayed, intimacy and connection go into free fall. It is, therefore, paramount to nurture trust in your relationship and to restore it when it has been damaged. The easiest and most powerful way to do this is to offer a sincere apology. An effective apology can go a long way toward repairing broken trust—even when a major breach has occurred.

As a therapist, I normally see couples in my office only when they are on the verge of breaking up. Most of the time, the basic issue is one of broken trust. Partner A thinks Partner B is untrustworthy in some way. Partner B thinks the same about Partner A. They each enter my office hoping I'll set the record straight by declaring the *other* person fully to blame and untrustworthy. Of course, I don't do that. Instead, I attempt to show both partners that they are each behaving in a way that interferes with establishing ongoing trust. While identifying these behaviors can be difficult, the remedy for restoring trust is relatively easy. It first involves apologizing for any hurt we may have caused our partners.

How do you feel about apologizing to your partner? Most people would rather be in a dentist's chair getting a root canal. Our egos hate to apologize. We think: "Why should *I* have to apologize after all *he* did to me?" Or: "Why should it be *me*? *She's* the one at fault." Well, the truth is that it always takes two to tango. Even if you feel you are the one who was wronged (and I'm sure you do), there's always *something* you could have done differently or better. A sincere apology opens the way for the restoration of trust and connection. In fact, apologizing is so powerful that it can literally overcome years of distrust and hurt. Unfortunately, we rarely get to see examples of effective apologies. They are hard to give. And they are even harder to carry through on. But when someone is incapable of giving a sincere apology, it makes the restoration of trust pretty much impossible.

While apologies are incredibly effective in restoring trust, not all apologies are created equal. If your partner just had an affair with your friend and he says in a cavalier manner: "Okay, I'm sorry. I shouldn't have done it. Are you happy now?" Well no, you would not be happy. Truly effective and sincere apologies must incorporate these four essential characteristics:

1. Sincere guilt or remorse
2. A new insight into the problematic behavior
3. Full responsibility for the problematic behavior
4. A promise to act differently in the future

When these four aspects of an apology all come together in the right way, a magical restoration of love can occur.

I had a couple in my office many years ago whose marriage

was saved by a very effective apology. After being caught with another woman, Kyle told his wife: "I have previously felt that being sneaky would get me what I want in life. I now see how misguided this was. My affair has deeply hurt you and our marriage, and I feel horrible for what I've done. Every morning I wake up with a terrible sense of guilt that follows me throughout the day. Although our marriage has had its problems over the years, it was my deceitfulness and behavior that really destroyed the trust we previously had. I am sincerely sorry for what I did. If, in time, you decide you want to try to save our marriage, I will do anything to help with that process. I love you and, from this day forward, I promise to be fully truthful with you about my feelings and actions." Long story short, this apology was the first step toward the restoration of their marriage.

Although a sincere apology can be extremely powerful, it can also be extremely difficult. It can be helpful to have a structure that makes apologizing easier. The "I regret . . . I apologize" exercise can provide a nonthreatening environment within which partners can work to resolve trust issues. The process is simple. One partner completes two sentence prompts: "When I think about our relationship, I regret . . ." and "I apologize for . . ." Then the other partner thanks them for their thoughts and completes the same two prompts. Here's how Jason and Jill handled this exercise:

> **Jason:** When I think about our relationship, I regret that I don't thank you enough for cleaning up after me. I apologize for leaving my laundry all over the floor—expecting you to pick it up without me saying anything or ever appreciating you for it.
>
> **Jill:** Thank you. (pause) When I think about our relationship, I regret that I almost never initiate sex with you. I

apologize for being stingy in my display of physical affection and putting you in the position of always having to ask for sex.

Jason: Thank you.

After a pause, they went on to the second round.

Jason: When I think about our relationship, I regret that I was late this last week when taking you out on our date. I apologize for being inconsiderate and not even texting you that I'd be fifteen minutes late.

Jill: Thank you. (pause) When I think about our relationship, I regret getting mad at you and saying hurtful things when you were late for our date. I apologize for letting my anger out—instead of being more vulnerable and simply telling you I felt hurt and then dropping it.

Jason: Thank you.

After two rounds, Jill and Jason both felt more confident in the other's love and gave each other a hug.

Couples who do this exercise on a regular basis find that it keeps their level of trust and connection at a high level. It's like taking your car in for periodic maintenance. The upkeep makes the ride smoother and helps prevent major breakdowns. Remember, practice makes perfect. Most couples reserve the power of an apology for those times when the whole relationship is on the verge of collapse. Since they are not used to apologizing, however, their attempts at an apology in times of crisis are frequently not very effective. But if you are well versed in the art of apologizing, your efforts will likely go better when you *really* screw up and need to apologize.

I Regret . . . I Apologize For . . .

Now that we've laid the foundation for the why and how of apologizing, here are instructions for the exercise:

1. Create a safe space with no distractions. Decide how many rounds you will perform—how many apologies each of you will give. Decide who will go first.

2. State that the intention of the exercise is to help create deeper trust, promote forgiveness when appropriate, and prevent resentments from undermining the connection between you.

3. Complete the first sentence prompt: "When I think about our relationship, I regret . . ." (say what you regret). Then complete the second prompt: "I apologize for . . ." (be as specific as possible about what you're apologizing for). If you feel called to say more about your feelings or your partner's feelings, you can do that as well—as long as you don't rationalize your behavior or become judgmental.

4. When the first partner is done apologizing, the second partner responds by simply saying: "Thank you."

5. The second partner then completes the same two sentence prompts. The partner who began responds with a simple: "Thank you."

When both partners have given an apology and both have responded, the first round is complete. If you have agreed to engage in additional rounds, repeat steps 3 through 5 until finished.

At the end of the exercise, if either of you feel a desire to talk more about the apologies offered, you can do so as long as both partners are willing. You can say something like: "Is it okay if I ask you some questions or we talk about what was brought up in the exercise?" If your partner agrees, then proceed. If not, take a break and try again another time. Whenever possible, formally end the exercise with a hug.

Whatever comes to mind as you do this exercise is a good issue to bring up and apologize for. You can bring up issues that happened a long time in the past, address persistent problems, or talk about specific recent events. Take your time with this. Don't rush it. Saying or hearing an apology can be intense. Give yourself or your partner time to sit with and really take in the words being expressed.

There is a part of us that always wants our partners to apologize for the many real and imagined offenses we hold against them. It can feel deeply satisfying to finally hear the words "I'm sorry"—especially when they're expressed with sincerity. But you have to be willing to express your own regrets as well. This exercise helps clear any stagnant energy or resentments between two people. What's left is a clean slate and an open, honest, and loving connection.

Simple and Easy Practice

Giving an apology outside a structure can be even more powerful than using the exercise just described, because the *timing* of an apology is an important part of its power. If you can apologize soon after you say or do something you regret, it has even more effect. For example, let's say you get upset and say something hurtful to your mate. It can be very powerful if, soon thereafter, you say: "I apologize. I just said something mean-spirited. I'm sorry if it hurt you and I regret saying it. I hope you can accept my apology." Apologies like this are rare and therefore more noticed, more admired, and more effective. If you find that you regret some word or action, complete the following sentence prompt: "I'm sorry. I regret having . . . (say what you regret). I hope you accept my apology." Then notice how things quickly change for the better.

Alternatively, try writing a note of appreciation and/or do something nice for your partner as a sign of your remorse. Learn what helps your partner forgive you, and make sure you use those behaviors when necessary.

CHAPTER 29

Take a Break

Have you ever been in a downward spiral with your partner? Have you ever been in a mood where virtually everything you or your partner says just makes things worse? When we're upset, we often go into fighting mode, and fighting mode is not a good time to communicate. The exercises in this book can help you get out of fighting mode and back on track, but sometimes—you just need to take a break. The exercise in this chapter gives you a simple and strategic way to take a break and avoid that downward spiral. In essence, it's an agreement between you and your partner to stop talking for a while and just take care of yourselves. I call it the Yellow Light, Red Light exercise. The word on the street is that this exercise has prevented a lot of collisions.

There are two basic ways to improve the quality of a relationship. The first is to increase the pleasure, intimacy, and fun that exist when the two of you are together. That's very important, and there are many methods in this book to do just that. The other approach is to decrease the pain, hurtful behavior, and arguing between the two of you. That's where the Yellow Light, Red Light exercise can be so valuable. If you get the knack of how to use this one simple technique, you may find that you immediately decrease your hurtful behavior and arguing by as much as 80 percent.

Besides helping to sidestep arguments, this exercise can help create a sense of safety for both partners. When we're really upset, we often say hurtful things that can destroy the trust in a relationship. Furthermore, it's not unusual for one partner to become afraid when the other gets very upset. By agreeing to take a break from frustration and anger and respecting that agreement, partners can back away from potentially treatening situations and reestablish trust and safety in the relationship.

Yellow Light, Red Light

As you may have guessed, the "yellow" and "red" lights of this exercise are metaphors for traffic lights. A yellow light means to slow down; a red light means to stop. Yellow lights indicate a need for caution; red lights are there to avoid a crash. The same is true in this exercise.

When you notice that you and your partner are starting to go down a dark path, you can simply say: "Yellow light." This means that you're worried about things spiraling out of control and feel the need for caution. To avoid this happening, you each agree to take a two-minute break from talking. What you do during your two-minute break is completely up to you. You can go into different rooms, you can take deep breaths, or you can even sit quietly and hold hands. Whatever you agree to do is fine—as long as you don't talk for two minutes. Once the two minutes are over, you can communicate once again. Hopefully, the momentum of irritation and frustration you were feeling will have dissipated by that time.

Sometimes, partners can get so upset with each other that a two-minute break simply isn't enough. Or you may forget to take a "yellow-light" break when things are going downhill, and you find yourselves screaming at each other. That's when red lights can be helpful. Calling a "red light" means you're required to take a break from each other for a *minimum* of an hour. If you want, you can agree that a "red-light" break lasts longer. But, at the very least, it must last for an hour. That means no contact and no talking. Use this period of time to calm down and take care of yourself. Go for a walk, watch a video, or engage in some other enjoyable activity. Hopefully, when you finally do resume communication, you'll be in a much better place to do so.

Part of this technique is the agreement that *either* person can say "yellow light" or "red light" at *any* time—and it must immediately be heeded by the other partner. This is not always easy. Sometimes we get caught up in our anger and frustration and just don't want to let go of it. At times like these, it can help to have an agreement about the penalties for yellow- and red-light violations. For instance, my wife and I have agreed that, if either of us talks after a yellow- or red-light request, we have to pay the other $1.00 for each word spoken. This helps us to respect each other's occasional need to call a halt.

It's important to come to a clear agreement with your partner as to what each light signifies *before* you begin to use this technique. I suggest to clients that a yellow light calls for a two-minute break without talking, while a red light calls for a minimum of an hour without talking. In general, it's good to call a yellow light before giving your partner a red light. Some couples find that, if they need to communicate something during "red-light time," it's okay to do so through writing. That's fine, as long as both partners agree to it beforehand.

While this method is incredibly simple, it is not easy to do. Although it only involves saying two words, neither you nor your partner will want to say or hear those two words or abide by them. After all, you only use them in the middle of a heated exchange. The part of us that gets into an argument with our mates does not like to be interrupted. It likes to argue—and it likes to be right. That's why it's important to discuss this exercise with your partner beforehand and come to an iron-clad agreement that violations will have agreed-upon consequences. If you do that, you'll find that two simple words are all that's needed to reduce your arguments drastically and change detrimental behavior. What could be simpler than a two-word technique to end all arguments? That's pretty magical.

Simple and Easy Practice

If you want a short, or even a longer, break from your partner during a stressful time, but you haven't discussed this method, you can simply say something like: "I want to really hear what you have to say, but I'm very stressed now. Let me take a ten-minute break and cool down, and then we can try to work through this again. Okay? I'll see you in ten minutes." Then leave the room and do whatever you need to do to calm down and take care of yourself for the amount of time you requested. When you're feeling more centered, you'll both be in a better position to resolve whatever issues led to your difficulties.

CHAPTER 30

Accentuate the Positive

Life is infinitely complex, but the human mind likes to keep things simple. We like to know who is right and who is wrong, who is good and who is bad. Of course, life is full of shades of gray, but we rarely see all those shadings. This tendency toward "black or white" thinking was useful way back in our evolutionary past. Today, however, it can lead to needless suffering. A simple antidote for this tendency is to ask the question: "What else could this mean?" When stressful situations arise, we tend to get locked into a single (often disempowering) point of view. By repeatedly asking yourself (or your partner) this simple question, you can start to see other possibilities. The broader your perspective, the smaller your suffering.

I once heard a friend convey a story that illustrates the power of this question. While in India, he witnessed an arrogant man who walked up to a famous guru and cynically said: "If you're so wise, why don't you teach me about the nature of heaven and hell."

The guru looked up and said: "Teach *you* about heaven and hell? I couldn't teach you anything. You're a cocky, narcissistic jerk. You're a complete moron; you're even repulsive to look at.

You don't have a caring bone in your entire body. Stop wasting my time and just get out of my sight."

Upon hearing these words, the man got red in the face and shook with rage. In a moment of pure hatred, he prepared to punch the guru in the face, but an instant before he threw his punch, the guru looked him straight in the eye and said: "That's hell."

The man suddenly realized that the guru had risked being beaten up just to teach him this lesson. He unclenched his fist, took a deep breath, and, in profound gratitude, bowed to the guru. And the guru said: "That's heaven."

This story clearly teaches that we create our own heaven and our own hell by how we see and interpret the events in our lives. The arrogant man in the story created a moment of pure hell for himself by interpreting the guru's comments in a negative light. He might have realized that the guru was teaching him a valuable lesson if he had only asked himself: "What else could this mean?" Of course, he might also have concluded that the guru was really just a mean person. Whatever his new interpretation, it probably would have been more empowering than his initial reaction. Indeed, when he finally *did* reinterpret the guru's words, it led to a deep feeling of gratitude.

A client of mine, Don, used this technique to head off a disaster on his honeymoon. He and his fiancé, Kara, had agreed to use this technique early in their relationship. While he was out picking up some food, Kara discovered that his smartphone had a text message on it: "How you doing lover boy? Love and kisses, Chris." She got livid, thinking to herself: "He's cheating on me on our honeymoon! That bastard!" By the time Don got back to the hotel, he found Kara packing to leave. He asked what was going on and, of course, got lambasted for being a lying, cheating blank blank blank. Once Don saw the message on his phone, he asked Kara: "What else could this mean?"

At first, Kara wouldn't answer the question, but they had an iron-clad agreement that they'd always come up with at least two answers if asked. Finally, she said: "It could mean that someone sent a text to the wrong phone number." Just this thought calmed her down quite a bit. Then Don asked: "And what *else* could it mean?" Kara answered: "It could mean that you have a relative named Chris who is asking how you are doing." After that, Kara calmed down enough so that Don could explain that Chris was a male friend at work with an irreverent sense of humor. In fact, Kara had met him at the wedding but hadn't put it together. Had it not been for Kara's agreement to answer that key question, she probably would have walked out on her own honeymoon.

You can use this technique to help ease tense and potentially damaging situations in your relationship. Just ask the key question: "What else could this mean?"

What Else Could This Mean?

We frequently interpret our partner's words and behavior in the worst possible way. This often leads to more upset than is called for. In chapter 2, we talked about the power of seeing your partner's positive intention. The question "What else could this mean?" can help you look for other—more positive—motivations behind your partner's words and actions.

The key to the success of this exercise is to make a firm agreement, *before* an argument or conflict arises, to come up with at least two answers to this question whenever your partner asks it of you. If you think it necessary, write this agreement down. You may be wondering, "Why not just point out to your partner how they are misinterpreting the situation at hand?" You could do this, but such feedback is rarely appreciated during a heated exchange. On the other hand, asking, "What else could this mean?" gently guides your partner to see things in a different way. Your agreement to come up with at least two answers to that question can save you a lot of trouble. Alternatively, when you're upset with something your partner said or did, ask yourself, "What else could this mean?" and see if this question can calm you down.

When we're very upset, it's usually because we've come up with a number of negative interpretations for what's happening. As we stack these negative thoughts on top of each other, we can become increasingly angry, depressed, or fearful. The antidote to these poisonous thoughts can be as simple as asking the question: "What else could this mean?" Of course, you have to be willing to come up with at least a couple of answers. Even if you don't really believe those answers, you'll give yourself a little space for new truths to be revealed. By making an agreement with your partner to use this exercise, you can insure yourself against volatile misunderstandings. Better yet, when you commit to using this question on yourself, you give yourself a quick way to overcome your own emotional upheaval.

Simple and Easy Practice

What if your partner has not read this chapter and you simply ask them: "What else could this mean?" They may not understand what you're talking about. In this case, you may want to rephrase the question and ask something like: "You seem upset by how you're viewing this situation. I'm wondering if there's another way to look at this. Could there potentially be anything good that comes from this, or any other way to see this?" If your partner can't see any other interpretations, ask them if it's okay if you mention a couple of other possible ways to see the situation. Once you get permission, you can share your own interpretations.

CHAPTER 31

Write What You Feel

Sometimes it can be helpful just to write a letter to your mate. This can simply be a heartfelt expression of what you're experiencing in your relationship, what you see happening, and what you really want. Many people write very differently from the way they speak. Moreover, people *receive* written communications in a manner different from the way they receive verbal communication.

There are four key elements to include in any letter you write to address a problem in your relationship:

1. Share your thoughts and feelings.
2. Identify the problem and what has contributed to it.
3. State what you want.
4. Suggest solutions to make things go better.

Magan had recently found out that her husband, Brent, was having an affair. She felt she wasn't ready to talk to him about it yet, because she was so overwhelmed, hurt, and confused. Instead, she decided to write a letter as a way of clarifying and communicating what she wanted to express. She used the four elements above to make sure that she said what she needed to say. Although the letter is brief, it contains a lot of useful information.

Dear Brent,

I'm feeling incredibly sad, hurt, angry, and fearful. The feelings come and go and change—like waves crashing against me. I'm thinking many contradictory thoughts: "Do I want to stay with you? What do we tell the kids who notice our distance? How was I to blame? How were you to blame? What can we do to make it all better?"

I see your affair as a symptom of a larger problem. We both have been preoccupied with work these last months, and not focused on truly connecting with each other. I've been overly critical of you, and I'm sure that hasn't felt good. You have avoided telling me what you're feeling and wanting, which eventually led to you wanting intimacy with another woman. There's plenty of blame to go around.

Ultimately, I want to repair our marriage. I want to have fun and feel close to you again. I want trust to be restored. I want us to enjoy the kids together like we used to. I want to let go of my being angry at you, and I want you to be honest and open with me.

We are clearly at a crossroad. I don't think we'll be able to get out of this mess on our own. I propose we find a marriage counselor who can help us return to a place of trust and connection. Even if counseling doesn't work, we'll at least know that we gave it our best try.

I am open to hearing what's going on with you, what you want, and any suggestions you have for moving forward.

Love,

Magan

Ultimately, this couple came to me for counseling and, after a few intense sessions, their trust, intimacy, and marriage were restored. Had Magan simply started screaming at Brent and blaming him for everything, the marriage would likely have ended. Fortunately, she decided to be vulnerable, choose her words carefully, and write down what she needed to say.

If you feel speaking from your heart is hard for you, writing may be particularly helpful. Try writing to your partner, and you may find that he or she is more receptive to what you have to say.

Dear John . . .

It's best to write your letter by hand or at least print it out from your computer and deliver it in person. Don't email it. People react differently to a letter that's handwritten or printed out than to something that's read on a screen. On the other hand, if you do write on a computer, you have the advantage of being able to edit your letter and revise it until it feels just right.

Remember to include all four elements given above. The following questions can help guide you:

1. What am I feeling and thinking?
2. How do I see the problem? How do I see myself contributing to it? How do I see my partner contributing to it?
3. What is it that I want?
4. What solutions and/or suggestions do I have to make things go better?

These questions are just guidelines to help you get started. It's *your* letter and your relationship, so write what feels true for you.

Simple and Easy Practice

Letter writing can also be useful in times other than a crisis. You can use letters or even short notes as an expression of what you love about your partner or as an update about what's going on with you. Sometimes I like to leave a note for my wife that says something like: "I'm excited to spend quality time with you tonight." If your partner reacts well to notes like this, write them more often.

P.S. Notes and letters with a cute P.S. at the end are especially endearing.

Conclusion

Final Thoughts

We've got this gift of love, but love is like a precious plant. You've got to keep watering it.

JOHN LENNON

We all want the same things in life and from each other. We want care, understanding, empathy, and appreciation. Yet couples who don't work on their communication often get lost in patterns of conflict that drain the love from their relationship. By picking up and reading this book, you've started a journey that can take you to ever-deepening levels of peace, connection, and intimacy. But it won't happen overnight. Learning any new skill takes practice. You need to learn which methods in this book really work best for you and, over time, become skilled in their use. Mastery is achieved when you have appropriate tools at your disposal and know how and when to use them. On the other hand, you will likely experience an immediate deepening of trust, care, and connection even the first time you use the exercises outlined here.

I devoted a lot of time in this book to describing specific guidelines and settings for each exercise because, over the years, I've learned that the structure and tone of communication greatly impacts its quality. With practice, however, you will learn to rely less on this structure and to use the methods in whatever way works best for you and your partner. As you become more skilled with these techniques, you'll find they naturally become part of the way you communicate in daily life.

Enjoy Each Learning Stage

No matter what the skill, we go through four distinct "stages" when learning to master any ability. In the first stage, you are unaware of how much you don't know: "Why would I need to read a book about communication? There's not much to know." By reading this book, you have officially completed this stage. Congratulations!

In stage two, you understand there's a lot to learn. This can be difficult, and many people lose courage here and give up. If you persist, however, you glide easily into phase three, in which, with some effort, you can begin to use your newfound skill to create the result you want. In stage four, you achieve what is called "unconscious competence." You become a master communicator—all without conscious effort. By being aware of the four stages of learning, you can get an overall perspective of where you are in the process and where you are headed.

Now I've got good news and bad news. The bad news is that you can't skip any of these stages. The good news is that, if you recognize the stages, it can be easier to progress along your path. For example, if you're now burdened with knowing that you're not skilled at advanced communication methods, you also know that it's just a matter of time until you will be much better. Allow yourself time to make mistakes and gradually improve. It will be worth it. True communication mastery is possible. You'll soon be able to communicate in a way that satisfies both you and all those you care for. But it won't happen if you don't give yourself time to practice and permission to make some mistakes along the way.

Around the year 1100, an unknown monk wrote:

When I was a young man, I wanted to change the world. I found it was difficult to change the world, so I tried to change my nation. When I found I couldn't change the nation, I began to focus on my town. I couldn't change the town and as an older man, I tried to change my family. Now, as an old man, I realize the only thing I can change is myself, and suddenly I realize that if, long ago, I had changed myself, I could have made an impact on my family. My family and I could have made an impact on our town. Their impact could have changed the nation, and I could indeed have changed the world.

By using the ideas and methods in this book, you can indeed change the world—or at the very least *your* world and the experience of the people you care about. Having read this book, you now know more about communication and relationships than 99 percent of the people around you. It is my hope you'll use your new understanding to inspire others to create more love and less conflict in their own lives. Telling others what you've learned here will reinforce your own knowledge and potentially help others to lead happier and less stressful lives as well.

Imagine a world in which everyone likes and respects you. Whether in your home, at your office, or while doing errands around town, everyone you see smiles at you and is happy to see you. They sense you are a loving, caring presence. It feels good to be in a constant state of connection with your intimate partner, as well as with all the people with whom you come in contact. People quickly come to recognize your "superpowers" of caring, understanding, and empathy. When you use the ideas and exercises in this book, before long, you won't have to imagine this scenario. You'll be living it.

APPENDIX A

Guide to Exercises

Below you will find very brief descriptions of the exercises in this book. Like a menu in a restaurant, you can browse this guide and find the item(s) that call out to you in the moment. Once you've tried a particular exercise, you'll have a better sense of what it can do for you and your partner. As you use these exercises, you will be well on your way to creating more love and less conflict in your relationship.

Part II: Understanding Your Partner

CHAPTER 6: "I'M JUST CURIOUS . . ."
To help couples know each other better and to prevent heated discussions from turning into arguments.

CHAPTER 7: "I'M FEELING . . . I'M WANTING . . ."
To encourage vulnerable communication; to help you know what you want and to move toward that experience with your partner.

CHAPTER 8: HOW DO I LOVE THEE?
To help partners know the key behaviors and activities that make each of them feel fully loved by the other.

CHAPTER 9: "I DON'T LIKE IT . . . I'D PREFER . . ."
To help couples know each other's most sensitive issues so they can avoid them and therefore have less conflict.

CHAPTER 10: TRIGGER QUESTIONS
To help partners become less reactive to things their mates say or do that bother them.

CHAPTER 11: THE NAKED TRUTH
To help couples know exactly what their partners like and dislike when having sex.

CHAPTER 12: MR. AND MRS. WONDERFUL
To help couples better understand what they really want from their partners and what their partners really want from them.

CHAPTER 13: PLAY TOGETHER; STAY TOGETHER
To help couples better know what activities they are most likely to enjoy together; to help them bond in a positive way through the power of humor and play.

CHAPTER 14: "IF YOU REALLY KNEW ME . . ."
To help couples connect quickly in a vulnerable manner and get to know their partners more intimately.

Part III: Increasing Love in Your Relationship

CHAPTER 15: "I NOTICE . . . I IMAGINE . . ."
To encourage couples to connect quickly and deeply and help them experience an empathic understanding that will avoid misunderstandings.

CHAPTER 16: "I APPRECIATE . . . THANK YOU"
A quick way to climb out of a relationship rut or negative cycle and to increase the good feelings you enjoy with your mate.

CHAPTER 17: "WHAT . . . ?"
Two groups of fifteen questions, the first aimed at increasing intimacy and the second aimed at increasing empathy.

CHAPTER 18: RELATIONSHIP TUNE-UP
To help couples know about their partners' inner world and connect in a quick, intimate manner.

CHAPTER 19: SPOON TUNE

To help couples feel emotionally connected without the use of words and to quickly overcome stress and irritation.

CHAPTER 20: THE HIGHER SELF

To help partners give permission to each other to give advice that can help them overcome problems and achieve greater perspective.

Part IV: Reducing Conflict

CHAPTER 21: SELF-EMPATHY PEP TALK

To help partners achieve a good state of mind to give or receive difficult communications so that things will go better between them.

CHAPTER 22:"WHAT I HEARD . . ."

To help partners listen empathically to each other, thereby fostering greater emotional connection and understanding.

CHAPTER 23: "HOW DID I CONTRIBUTE?"

To help couples overcome blame and avoid arguments by taking responsibility for behaviors that cause problems in their relationship.

CHAPTER 24: "YOU TALK . . . I'LL LISTEN"

To help partners feel better understood and to increase empathy and listening skills.

CHAPTER 25: "WOULD YOU LIKE TO HEAR . . . ?"

To help couples overcome blocks to intimacy and create a safe and vulnerable space for total honesty.

CHAPTER 26: SEARCHING FOR SOLUTIONS

To help couples overcome blame and find solutions to problems that are mutually beneficial and satisfying.

CHAPTER 27: "IF YOU'LL . . . THEN I'LL . . ."

To help couples make changes in problematic behaviors in ways that are mutually agreeable and foster a sense of fairness in the relationship.

CHAPTER 28: "I REGRET . . . I APOLOGIZE FOR . . ."

To help couples overcome blame, hurt, and resentments and bring them back to a place of deep emotional connection.

CHAPTER 29: YELLOW LIGHT, RED LIGHT

To help couples avoid arguments or downward spirals when stressed or dealing with sensitive topics.

CHAPTER 30: "WHAT ELSE COULD THIS MEAN?"

To help couples see alternative ways of interpreting behaviors or words to avoid misunderstandings, arguments, and negative feelings.

CHAPTER 31: "DEAR JOHN . . ."

To help couples overcome problems without verbal interaction and allow them to be more specific about what they are experiencing.

APPENDIX B

Lists of Emotions and Desires

Collected below are the lists of emotions and desires given in chapters throughout the book. These lists can be helpful in pinpointing your own feelings and those of your partner. Refer to the lists of positive and negative emotions whenever you need a more precise word to describe what you're experiencing and to help you name what you're feeling. Use the list of Fifty Universal Desires to pinpoint what you really want or whenever you feel uncertain about what you want. Refer to it to give you descriptive words to express what you truly desire.

Negative Emotions

Afraid	Agitated
Angry	Annoyed
Ashamed	Bitter
Confused	Depressed
Detached	Disappointed
Disgusted	Embarrassed
Exhausted	Fearful
Frustrated	Guilty
Hurt	Impatient
Jealous	Lonely

Miserable
Overwhelmed
Sad
Upset
Withdrawn

Mournful
Resentful
Suspicious
Weary
Worried

Positive Emotions

Affectionate
Appreciative
Cheerful
Curious
Enthusiastic
Fulfilled
Happy
Invigorated
Overjoyed
Refreshed
Relieved
Safe
Stimulated
Trusting
Wonderful

Amused
Calm
Content
Ecstatic
Excited
Grateful
Hopeful
Loving
Peaceful
Relaxed
Satisfied
Secure
Tender
Warm
Yearning

Fifty Universal Desires

Peace of mind	Safety
Security	Trust
Ease	Independence
Spontaneity	Humor
Joy	Pleasure
Affection	Closeness
Companionship	Intimacy
Love	Nurturing
Sexual Expression	Tenderness
Acceptance	Care
Compassion	Consideration
Empathy	Kindness
Respect	Transcendence
Understanding	Gratitude
Belonging	Cooperation
Equality/fairness	Partnership
Authenticity	Creativity
Integrity	Honesty
Self-care	Self-realization
Learning	Discovery
Challenge	Contribution
Exploration	Purpose
Beauty	Support
Faith	Presence
Inspiration	Mutual recognition

Key Questions and Sentence Prompts

Below are lists of the Deeper Intimacy and Empathic Understanding Questions discussed in chapter 17. Use the Deeper Intimacy and Empathic Understanding questions to open channels of communication between you and your partner. I've also included the Relationship Tune-up sentence prompts from chapter 18. Be sure to use them often to perform periodic maintenance on your relationship.

Deeper Intimacy Questions

1. What makes you feel most affectionate?
2. What was your first impression of me?
3. What do you like best about me?
4. What's one of your darkest secrets?
5. What do you want me to know about you?
6. What helps you to feel really loved?
7. What are you avoiding saying to me?
8. What do you notice about yourself when you're with me?
9. What was the last thing that made you cry? Why?
10. What frightens you about intimacy?
11. What's the most important thing you've learned about sex?
12. What do you think I think about you?

13. What makes you feel most connected to me?

14. What do you wish you could share with someone you love?

15. What do you feel right now?

Empathic Understanding Questions

1. What do you do to try to impress people or get them to like you?

2. What would your inner child say if he/she could speak?

3. What is something you've been learning about yourself?

4. What is your "superpower"?

5. What is your "kryptonite"?

6. What does a perfect day look like to you?

7. What do you feel the most gratitude for?

8. What is one thing you're ashamed of?

9. What is one thing you really "get" or understand about me?

10. What do you really like about yourself?

11. What was the most challenging time in your life? Why?

12. What is something you feel is missing in your life?

13. What event would you say shaped your life the most?

14. What is something that really scares you?

15. What makes you the happiest?

Relationship Tune-Up Prompts

1. The best thing that happened to me this week was . . .

2. Something I've been feeling lately is . . .

3. Something I've been wanting lately is . . .

4. The time I felt most connected to you recently was . . .

5. Something I appreciate about you (or have appreciated about you recently) is . . .

Acknowledgments

I want to thank Christine LeBlond for suggesting I do another book on communication and for offering great suggestions and editing all along the way. I also want to thank several friends who have taught me much about communication: Scott Catamas, Emily Orum, Tresa Yung, Kamala-Devi McClure, David Callendar, Simon Darcy, and Tamra Rutherford. Finally, I want to thank my wife, Kirsten, for lovingly showing me how I can always communicate even more effectively.

About the Author

 Photo by Jeannine Bordeaux

Jonathan Robinson is a psychotherapist, bestselling author of twelve books, and a professional speaker. He has reached over two hundred million people around the world with his practical methods and has made numerous appearances on the *Oprah* show and CNN, as well as other national TV talk shows. He has spent more than forty years studying the most practical and powerful methods for personal and professional development, and his work has appeared in *Newsweek, USA TODAY,* and the *Los Angeles Times,* as well as dozens of other publications.

Jonathan speaks regularly to Fortune 500 companies like Google, Microsoft, Dell, Bank of America, Coca-Cola, and FedEx. In his public talks and workshops, he is known for providing audiences with powerful and immediately useful information in a fun and entertaining manner. His other books include: *The Experience of God, Life's Big Questions, Instant Insight, Real Wealth, Communication Miracles for Couples, Shortcuts to Bliss, Shortcuts to Success, The Complete Idiots Guide to Awakening Your Spirituality, Find Happiness Now,* and *The Technology of Joy.* Jonathan is also the cohost of the podcast *Awareness Explorers.*

You can reach him by email at *iamjonr@aol.com* and find free articles, audio downloads, and information on his seminars on the web at *FindingHappiness.com* or *MoreLoveLessConflict.com.*

To Our Readers

Conari Press, an imprint of Red Wheel/Weiser, publishes books on topics ranging from spirituality, personal growth, and relationships to women's issues, parenting, and social issues. Our mission is to publish quality books that will make a difference in people's lives—how we feel about ourselves and how we relate to one another. We value integrity, compassion, and receptivity, both in the books we publish and in the way we do business.

Our readers are our most important resource, and we appreciate your input, suggestions, and ideas about what you would like to see published.

Visit our website at *www.redwheelweiser.com* to learn about our upcoming books and free downloads, and be sure to go to *www.redwheelweiser.com/newsletter* to sign up for newsletters and exclusive offers.

You can also contact us at *info@rwwbooks.com*.

Conari Press
an imprint of Red Wheel/Weiser, LLC
65 Parker Street, Suite 7
Newburyport, MA 01950
www.redwheelweiser.com